W9-AOD-550

COWLEY PUBLICATIONS is a ministry of the brothers of
the Society of Saint John the Evangelist, a monastic
order in the Episcopal Church. Our mission is to provide
books and resources for those seeking spiritual and theological formation. Cowley Publications is committed to
developing a new generation of writers and teachers who
will encourage people to think and pray in new ways
about spirituality, reconciliation, and the future.

becoming
human

To Betty
w/ much love,
from MOOOOOO + Harry

becoming human

Core Teachings of Jesus

Brian C. Taylor

Cowley Publications
Cambridge, Massachusetts

Library of Congress Cataloging-in-Publication Data
Taylor, Brian C., 1951–
   Becoming human : core teachings of Jesus / Brian C. Taylor.
       p. cm.
   Includes bibliographical references.
   ISBN 1–56101–257–2 (pbk. : alk. paper)
   1. Christian life—Biblical teaching. 2. Bible. N.T.
Gospels—Criticism, interpretation, etc. I. Title.
   BS2555.6.C48T29 2005
   248.4—dc22

                        2004030478

Scripture quotations are taken from *The New Revised Standard Version of the Bible*, © 1989, by the Division of Christian Education of the National Council of the Churches of Christ in the United States of America. Used by permission.

Cover design: Gary Ragaglia

Cowley Publications
4 Brattle Street
Cambridge, Massachusetts 02138
800-225-1534 • www.cowley.org

I offer this book in thanksgiving for the past, present, and future members of the community of St. Michael and All Angels Episcopal Church in Albuquerque, New Mexico. I have learned most of what I know about Jesus from our long walk together.

contents

contents

introduction

for those who are truly alive, life continually evolves. As Christians, our experience of God and our view of Jesus evolve, too.

Not so long ago, my awareness of God and Christ was centered in contemplative prayer. This is the place out of which I wrote my last book for Cowley Publications, *Becoming Christ: Transformation through Contemplation.*

For reasons beyond my comprehension or control, shortly afterward I evolved, quite surprisingly, away from the contemplative world in which I had been so immersed. I just couldn't read another book on prayer. My spiritual disciplines became a shambles. I lost connection with the word *spirituality*. I had seemingly been transformed by contemplation, but in a way that I could never have predicted. (Isn't that always the way?) It was a real loss, and I was at loose ends. Something had died.

At the same time, my interest in life began to grow. I've always known that God is fully immersed in everyday life, not encased in religion or spirituality, and in fact this view has been behind everything I've ever written. But now, I began to be able to find God *only* in life as it is: in family and friendships, quiet moments alone, meals, parish work, exercise, music, in the intensity of life's challenges, in my everyday consciousness, even in the struggle to move beyond those ways in which I habitually keep myself limited and apart from God. I began to actually live that which is the essence of all forms of spirituality: an immersion in the everyday activities of life.

The ordinary now seemed quite *enough*, without adding what felt like an artificial layer of "spirituality" on top of it. I still prayed, but now in a way that arose naturally out of whatever circumstance I was in. To use an analogy I've mentioned in this book, it was as if the training wheels just fell off, and I discovered that I was riding the bike, which is life in God.

Jesus then came to the fore, in a new way. His teachings have always been central in my adulthood, but now something was different. There was a fresh, immediate, liberating quality to what he had to say about life. His guidance about *how to live* struck me to the core. One morning I spent a few hours leafing through the gospels, jotting down his teachings about relationships, the world, God, and human consciousness in the most succinct and accurate terms I could come up with: *Don't worry; Love everybody; Help the poor; Die to yourself; Don't be too religious; Become simple; Face into conflict; Change the world; Forgive yourself for being human . . .*

These phrases became this book. In between that morning perusal of the gospels and the completion of this collection of short chapters, I have been repeatedly reminded of Jesus' astonishing perspective on this human life. In his lifetime, it was this perspective that transformed those who had the ears to hear him, so much so that they dropped everything and became his followers. His perspective still astonishes and transforms those who have ears to hear him.

As we follow Jesus, we will find that he helps us to become human, truly and fully human. In his fellowship, we become the creatures that our Creator intends us to be. In Jesus, God became fully human, in order to show us how to do the same. As the second-century bishop Irenaeus of Lyons puts it, "The glory of God is the human person fully alive."

become simple

technology, communication, and our modern economy have brought some of us many very good things. We can travel to indigenous jungle cultures or the far-off desert in a day or two or we can communicate by e-mail with a friend in another continent. We have access to wonderful anti-anxiety and blood-thinning medications, organic coffee from cooperative plantations, and digital music devices that enable us to hold our entire music library in the palm of our hand. Discussions on television shows expose us to new ways of thinking about previously forbidden family constructions, and our cities and suburbs are populated with Jamaicans and Nigerians and Koreans and everyone else.

We live in an increasingly complex environment. At times we're bewildered by moral choices that seem ever more gray and uncertain, such as those presented by stem-cell research or new definitions of gender identity. We're faced with a fast pace of living all around us that sucks us into its vortex—running from commitment to recreation to responsibility to entertainment so quickly that we wear ourselves out. Problems that have always vexed the world—hunger, poverty, disease, war, crime, pollution—now have become so complicated and dangerous that solutions seem impossible. We are working harder, more in debt, making ourselves unhealthy, becoming ever more dependent upon mood-altering drugs, and all the while sensing that the world around us is spinning out of control.

We know that a spiritual life helps us to cope with the complexity of our lives. Meditation and prayer relieve stress, we find support for our lives through relationships in community, and many are comforted by the traditional messages of hope in scripture: "The Lord is my shepherd, I shall not want" (Psalm 23:1).

But a spiritual life also promises something more radical, in the true sense of the word: that is, *going to the root, the core*. Spirituality offers the possibility that we can actually become free from the destructive energy of a stressed-out life. Spirituality promises a kind of simplicity in the midst of our complex world.

We long for spiritual calm in the middle of the storm, for a humble, human existence that is grounded, sane, and real. We wonder whether we will ever be able to create or return to a pace of living that is more natural. Remembering our childhood, a vacation, retreat, or even just imagining a more ideal time and place, we wonder how things ever got so crazy, and whether it is even possible to change what we have become accustomed to.

My generation tried to make this return to sanity of lifestyle in a back-to-the-land movement in the late 1960s and early '70s. Thousands of us raised our own vegetables, baked our own bread and made our own music, shopped in thrift stores, worked part-time (if at all), and tried to become as self-sufficient as possible. We dropped out of the world of consumerism and stressful jobs. We strove to be counter-cultural, so that we might undo a pattern of living that a Navajo friend of mine described by saying, "White people have all the watches, but Indians have all the time."

But for most of us, dropping out is not the answer. Trying to become an anti-technology Luddite in the midst of our world as it is today is not only difficult, it can be a simplistic and artificial response. For most of us the answer to our complex lives does not lie in rejecting the world and taking on a utopian lifestyle. Most of us will continue to pay a mortgage, drive a car, work with telephones and computers, and have to deal with all the difficulties and joys of modern life. I believe that the spiritual answer to the stressful and destructive complexity of our world is more subtle, and is both internal and external. It has to do both with our consciousness and the way we live.

First, we can change our perspective from within. We can seek an inner simplicity, a way of slowing down and humbling our consciousness so that we are more integrated and awake. Through meditation, we might learn how to become more present to and happy with the simple and concrete things of life: the weather, our food, our breath, the moment at hand. This helps us to be less mentally caught up in the busyness and imagined importance of what we are doing, so that we can simply go through our day, doing what we have to do, but remaining present and simple as we do everything.

This is what Jesus intended when he called a child forward and said to his disciples, "Truly I tell you, unless you change and become like children, you will never enter the kingdom of heaven" (Matthew 18:3). Listen to what he is saying: you will never enter the divine dimension unless you change and become like a child. But what does this mean?

We know that it doesn't mean that we become childish, that we return to innocence, where there are no problems, no responsibilities. We are to be in the world, engaged with its concerns as people of faith. St. Paul spoke of becoming spiritually mature, where he "put an end to childish ways" (1 Corinthians 13:11). Becoming like a child may mean rather that we reclaim a certain openness to the moment, a playful sense of appreciation and wonder. It certainly means that we have a humble frame of mind which seeks and finds contentment in the small things. And it means that we develop the capacity to leave behind those things that we don't really have to carry into every moment: our responsibilities, worries, and ambitions. We don't *have* to hold in the back of our mind all those little things at work we have yet to accomplish, and we *can* remember to look up at the sky or even down at the marvelous bubbles in the dishwater.

Meditation is perhaps the most effective way of developing this capacity. In sitting quietly, we learn how to slow down our mind and be present through our senses. We learn about those persistent habits of emotion and thought that tend to grip our consciousness, and we learn how to extricate ourselves from their control over us. For instance, our anger toward others who oppose those things we want to accomplish at work becomes evident in the "distractions" of meditation, and this awareness helps us to be free from the grip of this otherwise unconscious emotion. For those who are not inclined toward a still, contemplative practice of prayer, a simple, open heart can be developed through focused activity such as practicing a musical instrument or taking walks outdoors.

Whatever we do in order to find this inner simplicity, it has become even more necessary in our modern age than it was in Jesus' own time. We will not, in fact, enter that quality of life Jesus called "the kingdom of heaven" without becoming more like a child: by slowing down, waking up, and experiencing life less mentally and stressfully than we normally do.

The other part of becoming simple is external. It has to do with the everyday choices we make about how to live. We can choose to be less driven by our consumer culture and less submissive to the frantic pace of life that surrounds us. We can say no to that second invitation to dinner on a weekend, decide not to take on that new volunteer commitment, or limit the number of extra-curricular activities our children sign up for. But doing so means that we will have to become counter-cultural to some extent; we'll have to be intentionally uncooperative with the forces that push us all along.

We really don't have to do as much as most of us do. We can politely decline some of the demands on our time, and devote more of our time to gardening or reading. We can spend less money on—and time shopping for—clothes, gadgets, decorations, and other products that seem to promise stimulation and fulfillment, but which only, in reality, deplete and diminish us. My own tendency on weekends is to seek out companionship and entertainment as a release from the work week, only to find that these pursuits sometimes just tire me out; what I really need is rest. At a deep level, saying no to these activities is really saying no to the illusion of satisfaction that will be supposedly found in activity and consumption. This helps us to look for our fulfillment in smaller and more humble things. This is truly counter-cultural, and the intentional choice for it must be made every day.

Jesus supported an intentional, counter-cultural external simplicity in many of his teachings. He told us that our servitude to money would always hinder our efforts to seek God. He pointed out the absurdity of a man who wore himself out working and saving and putting away security for himself, only to die anyway and lose it all. And in the most poignant passage of all, Jesus said:

> . . . do not worry about your life, what you will eat or what you will drink, or about your body, what you will wear. Is not life more than food, and the body more than clothing? Look at the birds of the air; they neither sow nor reap nor gather into barns, and yet your heavenly Father feeds them. Are you not of more value than they? And can any of you by worrying add a single hour to your span of life? And why do you worry about clothing? Consider the lilies of the field, how they grow; they neither toil nor spin, yet I tell you, even Solomon in all his glory was not clothed like one of these. But if God so clothes the grass of the field, which is alive today and tomorrow

is thrown into the oven, will he not much more clothe you—you of little faith? Therefore do not worry, saying, "What will we eat?" or "What will we drink?" or "What will we wear?" For it is the Gentiles who strive for all these things; and indeed your heavenly Father knows that you need all these things. But strive first for the kingdom of God and his righteousness, and all these things will be given to you as well. (Matthew 6:25–33)

Jesus taught several important things about simplicity in this part of the Sermon on the Mount. First of all, it is the worries about food and clothing and time that consume and destroy us, not the things or the activities themselves. It is also the desire for these things that causes us to chase after them. After all, birds of the air and lilies of the field don't crave products and experiences; they're happy with the richness and beauty of life as it already is. What God provides for us is normally more than enough. True satisfaction is found as we learn to be content with what we have, and not, out of a chronic sense of vague dissatisfaction, constantly extend ourselves forward into what we might yet have, and what we imagine it might do for us.

Jesus said "unless you *change and become* like children," not "unless you *are* like a child. . . ." Internal and external simplicity are things that come only through a process of change and becoming. We can't just decide today that we will henceforth be simple, humble, and free. It is not easy to learn simplicity, for our attachments and fears and ambitions keep us enslaved. For instance, I tend to be enslaved, in a way, to a rather frenetic pace of working. And so I have to learn continually the lesson that I don't have to work lots of extra hours to please every person who wants my attention now, that I don't really have to get everything done exactly when I said I would. Only when we admit and release these kinds of attachments can we feel satisfied with a simpler, slower, more humble lifestyle. Only then can we feel fulfilled by just sitting still, appreciating the world as it is.

Thus the spiritual life is a process of subtraction more than addition. Rather than seeing religion only as an accumulation of various practices and virtues, it is also a matter of dropping those things that ultimately don't satisfy, and just being open in a simple way, gambling that this vulnerability will not disappoint us. On faith we must bank on the possibility that God will provide for us all that we need, that life itself—as it is—will not only feed us, but clothe us in glory. Learning that we can trust in this possibility, we become more simple, more like children in this respect, more like birds and lilies.

plant, water, and wait

a s part of a community that lived a rural life, Jesus and his disciples were in close contact with the earth and with farming. They understood how one must cooperate with the natural cycles of weather and the needs of the land in order to produce fruit and crops.

And so one time Jesus used a particular farming parable to teach something important about the relationship between our efforts and God's grace: "The kingdom of God is as if someone would scatter seed on the ground, and would sleep and rise night and day, and the seed would sprout and grow, he does not know how" (Mark 4:26–27).

Now the interesting thing about this parable is that it points out the obvious. We scatter seed, we plant and water, but do we really know *how* it sprouts and grows? Of course, we can give a biological explanation, or we can film it and then speed up the film so that we can see it, but really, do we understand how God makes something dry and seemingly dead into something living? Can you see the miraculous, divine energy of life itself enter into a dry seed so that it becomes a green living thing?

The only thing you can see is the *effect* of this miracle as it becomes a plant. You plant and water, you sleep and rise night and day, and the seed sprouts and grows and we don't know how. And yet it does. What does this tell us about the gifts of the Spirit, which we all desire? It tells us that we cannot make them ourselves. We don't stand over a seed we've just planted and shout at it, "Grow! C'mon now, move it! Become a tomato!" And neither need we stand over ourselves and force ourselves to be a better person, to be more wise, faithful, loving, peaceful, patient, kind, generous, gentle, and self-controlled. These are gifts, fruits of the Spirit; they come as the natural byproduct of a life of faith.

But the parable of the mysterious growth of the seed tells us more if we reflect on it further. For when we garden, we do have to be active. We may not be able to shout a tomato into existence, but we have to work for something to happen. It's like the story of a man on a walk who strolled through his neighborhood and saw a woman in her front yard, tending a lovely flower garden. The man commented, "Ah, the beauty of God in creation!" To which the woman replied, "Huh! You should have seen it when God tended this garden alone. It was a weedy mess!"

Likewise, for our spirits to flourish we take an active role also in the tending the garden of our souls. But what is that role, if not to make ourselves into better people?

We begin by creating a hospitable environment, a way of life that will be conducive to the Spirit's growth. For some of us, this might involve choosing to turn the television off more often, not automatically turning on the radio in our car, clearing out the clutter in our house, screening telephone calls, and finding other creative ways of maintaining a quieter and more peaceful atmosphere around us. Others of us might need an atmosphere of stimulation and creative engagement with people and activity. But the first step is to sustain a healthy environment that is conducive to the particular ways that the Spirit moves in us. And this is not a one-time decision that sets the proper environment in place; it has to be chosen every day.

Then we need to plant a seed. What is that seed? It is the kernel of hope we carry within us. It is the seed of our intention and our desire for a godly life. This is the potential that God has given us, and which can be planted every day. My own intention for the day is in the form of morning prayer, where I go over those things I'll be doing and the people I will be seeing, asking for God's grace to be present and open to the Spirit in all things. As Jesus said, all we need is a small bit of faith intention, no bigger than a mustard seed, and the kingdom of God, the Spirit, will grow it into a large bush. So, daily we hold before God our willingness to be available for the work of the Spirit, to listen, and to respond as best we can. This intention, this daily planting of the seed is important, for it sets the tone and begins the process every day.

We then dig in manure, that is, the real stuff of life: our dark side, our spiritual failure, our annoyingly habitual faults, whether they be resentment toward others, lack of devotion, self-indulgent appetites, or perfectionism. We tend to think that we're supposed to get rid of these things and then present ourselves as proper and pure before God. But the Spirit needs us to be real. The manure of our lives should not be hidden from God; it should be dug into our souls so that its nutrients can help produce needed growth.

While we may think of these things as "negative," "ungodly," or "shameful," they are the very things that provide spiritual nutrients for growth. Why? Because they make us humble, human, *humus*, of the earth; they teach us to be dependent upon God, to know that we are always beginners. If we are honest about ourselves, if we admit our shortcomings and our resistance, if we dig these things into our spiritual life, the soil will be much richer and earthier than if it is nourished only with sweet piety and affected goodness. An alcoholic who knows his capacity for destructive addictive behavior also knows his dependence upon God; similarly, an acute awareness of our irritation with those whose personalities annoy us will tend to make us similarly humble and dependent upon God.

Then we water our spiritual life with prayer and worship

and study and reflection. For each of us, this means different things. For some, it is the daily office, reading through the assigned psalms and lessons from scripture. For others, it is a quiet cup of coffee in the garden, a walk with the dog, an AA meeting, a book, an occasional retreat, or regular silent meditation. We don't have to be able to feel the results of doing this every day, any more than we have to have a special experience when we water the roses. We just have to water the seed of our intention. And we have to water it frequently, in anticipation of the Spirit's needs, not waiting until we are spiritually parched and withered up.

And finally we weed out foreign objects from time to time, so that there is room for the Spirit to grow. This is the work of repentance, of turning away from what is harmful to and in competition with the work of the Spirit in us. Actions have consequences, and when we discover that we've done things that violate the Spirit of Christ within, they take up room, they take up energy. And so we must do some weeding. The point here isn't to expect ourselves to be entirely free of weeds forever, and then feel ashamed and disappointed when we discover the little buggers shooting up again. Just weed again, that's all, tomorrow and the next day, and the day after that.

What can we expect will happen if we engage in this kind of spiritual gardening? When we set out to grow a garden, we know what kind of flower and fruit the seeds will produce. Just as we can be confident that the little dry seeds we plant and the preparation of the ground and the watering and all the rest will result in tomatoes or lettuce or corn, so the fruits of the Spirit are entirely predictable: wisdom, love, patience, kindness, generosity, self-control. What a relief this is when we really understand it! For then we can concentrate on the humble work that we *can* do: soul gardening. And we can allow the Spirit to do the work that she does: producing spiritual fruit.

So forget about trying to make yourself a good person. That's the Spirit's work, not yours! Focus instead on the kind of atmosphere the Spirit needs to grow in your life. Focus on the seed, that is, your faith and your intention to be available for the work of the Spirit. Focus on the kinds of things that nurture the growth of the Spirit for you. Dig in your struggles, the real stuff of life. Weed out anything that hinders this growth.

You will turn around one day and notice that you have become more Christ-like, that the Spirit, in fact, has been growing in the night when you weren't looking. You will discover more love and forgiveness, more patience, and more generosity. You will grow in wisdom and peace and self-control. And you will know that all of this is the work of the Spirit, who wants to make of our lives a beautiful garden for God.

change the world

*d*on't mix politics with religion. Respect the separation of church and state. Leave economic and social issues alone; stick to faith and prayer. Don't meddle in the affairs of the world.

We still hear these messages from voices within and without the church. Many churches and clergy act as if it were the gospel. Charity is fine. No problem there. Feed the hungry, clothe the naked, visit the sick, as Jesus instructed us. Just don't challenge the status quo. As the late Dom Helder Camara, a Brazilian archbishop, once lamented, "When I feed the hungry, they call me a saint; but when I ask why they're hungry, they call me a communist."

Attempting to change the world is controversial. Most of us are much more comfortable with charity. And in fact, charity does tremendous good. The poor need food. It is good to feed them. And it feels good to feed them. But wouldn't it be much better if they weren't hungry in the first place?

The other problem with a charity-only approach to the woes of the world is that it can inadvertently lead the charity-giver into pride, power, and paternalism. One of the motivations for helping all the "little people" is that it makes one feel so big and generous. This feeling of magnanimity is dependent upon there being others who will continue to be small and needy. It may be unconscious and unintended, but the net result of giving charity and *not* changing the world to promote more justice and equality is that the pressure is taken off everyone, so that the status quo can continue.

A story from nineteenth-century England illustrates this principle graphically. Some miners had been used to terrible wages, long hours, and dangerous working conditions. Those in the upper class in their vicinity had been used to helping the poor miners' families with boxes of food. In fact, among the donors were some of the wives of the very mine managers who were doing the exploiting. The miners went on strike, demanding change. The irony of the situation was highlighted by a banner they carried in the march: "Damn your Charity—we want Justice!"

We in the church have supported this social tendency, contributing to the pride, power, and paternalism of its privileged and charitable members. We have encouraged much in the way of charity—a good thing—but we have also discouraged anything that would rock the boat. Historically, this has been a survival strategy. As long as the church didn't make trouble for the state, the church would prosper and share in the benefits of power, wealth and property. Latin American clergy and bishops, such as the martyr Oscar Romero of El Salvador, have paid the price for turning their backs on the oligarchy and proclaiming a church that exercises God's biblical *preferential option for the poor*. There is still tremendous resistance to their perspective, as both church and state have found their ways of silencing or getting rid of them.

The worst part about this historic resistance of the church has been that it has silenced even Jesus. In our hymns, prayers, and sermons we portray him as an inoffensive, kindly, and soft man who cares only about healing the sick, welcoming children, forgiving every sin, and going humbly and silently to his death when he was faced with the powers of the world. Yet Jesus did and was so much more.

More than anything else Jesus said or did, he proclaimed

and modeled a kingdom of God, a kingdom of heaven that confronted the kingdoms of this world. Jesus would never have been crucified had he only been loving and kind. He was a threat because he proclaimed God's kingdom over and above the authority of both the Roman Empire and the Temple system. After all, he called for his disciples to have ultimate allegiance to a kingdom that was "not of this world." What was this kingdom that he proclaimed?

To show what it was, he broke social barriers and taboos by the way in which he lived. He gathered and fed, touched and healed rich, privileged, and "righteous" people right alongside the poor and outcast and "unclean." More important, he treated them as equals. But the really outrageous thing was that he told everyone and acted as if the despised and unsavory ones were actually ahead of the upright and privileged in God's kingdom. He portrayed this surprising social order as divine and eternal reality, in stark contrast to the temporary social illusion we construct in this world.

"So the last will be first, and the first will be last" (Matthew 20:16). "Blessed are you who are poor. . . . Blessed are you when people hate you, and when they exclude you. . . . But woe to you who are rich. . . . Woe to you when all speak well of you. . . ." (Luke 6:20, 22, 24, 26). The weak and vulnerable children, those with mental and physical disabilities, and the poor were all drawn into his circle and given an honored place at the table. A woman known to be a public "sinner" was allowed to touch Jesus, intimately washing his feet with her tears and drying them with her hair, right in front of the upright Pharisees: in their very house, no less (Luke 7). Jesus had intruded into the inner sanctum of social decorum with an upside-down social order.

Jesus was just as willing to heal the servant of a Roman soldier as the child of a poor peasant woman. He made no distinctions according to class or religious caste. The only thing that distinguished one person from another was the state of their heart, which was transparent to Jesus. Were their hearts, like his, centered in love, forgiveness, humility, and devotion to God? Or were they caught in social prejudice, pride, power, position, and privilege? Asking these questions, living as if they were the only ones that mattered, Jesus challenged and shocked the political and religious world of his day. This lifestyle and proclamation of the kingdom of God, so central to Jesus' whole mission, were both intended and understood to be a direct assault on the kingdom of Rome and the Temple elite, on the very structure of society itself.

But the thing that really got him in trouble, the thing that perhaps led the powerful to plot and execute his death, was his entrance into the temple in Jerusalem (Mark 11:12–18). His angry display of scattering money and overturning tables is not just a commentary on commercialism in a house of worship. It is an act of civil and religious disobedience, a disruptive protest that attacks the economic and political balance that temple and society had so carefully worked out. It is an intrusion of the kingdom of God into the kingdom of the world.

Money-changers provided the necessary animals for sacrifices required of religious pilgrims. From all over the Mediterranean, poor people came along with the rich, and they had to make their purchase in temple coinage, not the "unclean" money that they brought with them from their countries of origin. In this transaction, officials took advantage of the pilgrims, and money-changers made out like bandits as the poor made do with what they could. They had to offer high-priced pigeons for sacrifice instead of even more expensive lambs. All in the name of God. The Roman soldiers guarded the scene from a distance, in cooperation with the temple police within the compound. The whole system supported the temple elite, who supported Herod the Jewish puppet king, who supported Pilate the Roman governor. Everything worked in concert to uphold a stratified social system.

Jesus said no. He turned the tables. His actions set the

wheels in motion that would lead quickly to his arrest, mock trial, torture, and execution. He was a martyr because he challenged the status quo.

In the light of our Savior's social message, how are we called to be in the world? How are we called to follow Jesus? Clearly, charity is not enough. We are called to do what our Lord did, to set about changing the world so that it more closely resembles the kingdom of God.

And so: Work for medical care for all, whether or not they can afford it. Strive diligently toward true equality, respect, and employment for all races, classes, and conditions of people. In your church, make sure that people of color, women, those who are poor or working class are visible at the altar and in positions of leadership. Question your own tendency to be more enthusiastically welcoming at coffee hour toward the potential new member who is a well-dressed professional than you are to one who is poor and uneducated. In your place of business and in your church, pay employees decently and give them the same health and pension benefits as those in management, including your clergy. Challenge federal and state policies and systems that keep people powerless and take away their pride. Defend the vulnerable. Protect the earth from exploitation and pollution. Resist nationalistic tendencies toward fear, war, and the demonization of our enemies. Minister *with* the needy to empower them to address their own real needs, instead of ministering *to* them. Work with your church outreach programs to see if they can broaden their concerns—from charity to justice and advocacy—to benefit those whom they serve. Intrude upon the kingdom of the world with the kingdom of God. Change the world.

don't worry

Optimists say everything always works out for the best. But those who have suffered are skeptical about this piece of wisdom. How does a mother who is about to lose a child to a brain tumor respond when she is told, "Don't worry, everything will be fine, if you just have faith?" Everything doesn't always work out well. Just call to mind war, crippling poverty and disease, debilitating depression, and suicide. Or recall that we worship a man who was betrayed, abandoned, and who died a premature death hanging on a cross. In this life, things didn't work out so well for Jesus.

And yet, Jesus kept saying, in one way or another, that all would be well. "Do not worry about your life. . . . can any of you by worrying add a single hour to your span of life?" (Matthew 6:25, 27). To a synagogue ruler whose daughter had died, Jesus said, "Do not fear, only believe" (Mark 5:36). St. Paul, steeped in the Spirit of Jesus, said confidently: "We know that all things work together for good for those who love God" (Romans 8:28). How do we square these words with the reality of our lives, even with the reality of Jesus' life?

I don't think that it's just a matter of believing harder. The answer doesn't lie in forcing oneself to overcome common sense and natural fear about danger with grim certitude. Faith like this is brittle, hard. It projects itself outwards upon all who doubt, like a defensive weapon.

Neither does the answer lie in adopting a passive attitude of nonchalance. Bobby McFerrin parodied this stance—and the well-known slogan of Meher Baba, an Indian guru in the 1960s—in his catchy and delightfully insipid song "Don't Worry, Be Happy." The rent is late, the landlord says he's going to litigate, but don't worry, be happy! Clearly, there are things in life worth worrying about and then acting upon.

Jesus was concerned about people's health, happiness, and how we treat one another. We also need to be concerned about many things. But we tend to transform concern into anxiety, and carry around a little tightness in the chest, a fluttery stomach, headaches, a rushed pace, a heightened state of alertness or need to control even when it is not necessary. We are like Martha of Bethany, who, instead of taking the remarkable opportunity to pay attention to Jesus when he taught in her house, was completely stressed out, bustling around the kitchen, angry at her sister for not helping. She was "worried and distracted by many things" (Luke 10:41). To Martha and to us, too, Jesus speaks of the one thing that is necessary: *faith.*

While faith may not protect us from ever having to worry about the things that are going very badly in our lives, and while it may not make us blissfully passive, it does do two very important things. In the short run, faith brings a kind of equanimity to the ups and downs of life, replacing anxiety with trust. And in the long run, faith assures us with a confidence that even if things do go terribly wrong, ultimately all *will* be well in God. Even if we lose someone we love deeply and grieve their loss for years, life has a way of eventually bringing us new relationships, or perhaps a move to a more suitable home or a more creative job.

Equanimity is one of the fruits of a life that is given to faith, worship, and prayer. We go through our difficulties, small and large, and take our troubles to God. We learn that we must ask not for a specific outcome, but for God's will to be done, for the highest good to be served. In this prayer and faith, we gradually move into the experience of trust: not the kind of trust that something in particular will happen, but a purer form of trust: just trust. Be confident that you live in God, and no matter what happens or doesn't happen, you still live in God and life will still be good. This brings equanimity, the "peace of God which surpasses all understanding," as St. Paul put it (Philippians 4:7).

This peace indeed passes human understanding, for it isn't even linked to circumstances. It just is. Whether things are going well or not, faith helps us carry a sense of well-being around inside. This doesn't mean that we won't continue to feel fear or other human emotions. It means that when the fear arises, we have a way of facing it, transforming it into something other than control or anxiety.

Prayer and worship are the tools that we use to build faith when we get knocked around by life's circumstances. A moment of silent longing toward the Spirit will lift us out of our troubles and remind us of the goodness of this moment, this life. Singing a hymn with abandon, together with our community of faith, will enlarge our heart and fill us with hope. These experiences give us equanimity and peace, at times, in the short run.

In the long run, faith gives us the confidence that come what may, ultimately all will be well in God. Even if your son goes to war, even if you find yourself divorced, even if your best friend is diagnosed with cancer, even if your house is broken into and they take everything of sentimental value, love and life will eventually triumph. It will triumph not only for each of us personally, but also for all humanity, all creation. This is the promise of the resurrection, and the happy ending of scripture's story. It is the ultimate ground of reality that gives the saints a joy that cannot be shaken. We may not see the outcome of this victory in our lifetime, but our faith tells us of its promise.

Who will separate us from the love of Christ? Will hard-
ship, or distress, or persecution, or famine, or nakedness,
or peril, or sword? . . . No, in all these things we are more
than conquerors through him who loved us. For I am
convinced that neither death, nor life, nor angels, nor
rulers, nor things present, nor things to come, nor
powers, nor height, nor depth, nor anything else in all
creation, will be able to separate us from the love of God
in Christ Jesus our Lord. (Romans 8:35, 37–39)

Ah, to be convinced of this, as Paul was, as Jesus was! For
even as he approached his inevitable suffering and death in
Jerusalem, even while he agonized in Gethsemane in fear of
death, Jesus seemed to carry within himself a confidence that
in God, all would be well. I don't believe that this confidence
was the result of an inhuman prescience about his own resurrection to come. It was the result of faith. Grounded in something other than the circumstances of this life, grounded in
God's eternal being, Jesus could, at least at times, rest in the
knowledge that surpasses all understanding.

How is faith learned? How do we give things over to God
in prayer so that we can step out of anxiety into equanimity?
How do we live in the ultimate security and joy that in God all
will be well?

For some, faith is easy. They learned it very early in life, because they were lucky enough to have entered into a safe and
loving family environment. In the first year of life, the primary
lesson we learn from life is whether or not it is to be trusted.
This lesson stays with us, coloring our emotions, our outlook
and our faith—or lack thereof—for the rest of our lives.

For those who learn early on that life is not safe, not to be
trusted, faith must be learned the hard way. For them, faith
comes by faithing; the Greek New Testament word for *faith* is
a verb, after all, not a noun. It is something we must do, not
something we either have or don't have. Like muscles, faith

must be exercised in order to grow. Even those who begin with some faith must grow it through exercise. We faith every time we risk trusting instead of falling back into fear and control. We faith every time we abandon our usual coping mechanisms and rely instead on some unseen presence we can only dimly feel or understand.

Over time, this act of faithing builds trust. For we learn through our own experience that God can be counted on, if not to make things turn out just the way we want them to, at least to calm our heart and to bring good out of ill. We learn that God does give us a measure of joyful equanimity as we live a life of prayer, trust, and worship. It may sound simplistic, there are times when we cannot feel it, and it is difficult to gain, but these words are true: Do not worry about your life; all things work together for good for those who love God.

purify your heart

Our nation may have been founded by broad-minded Deists, but deep in our psyche are the witch hunts, *The Scarlet Letter,* and the Puritans. We still retain something of this legacy. "Sinners" are still shunned, and personal moral uprightness is all-important. We are horrified by a public leader who engages in private adultery. On the other hand, we consider as "highly principled" one who attends prayer meetings and would never cheat on his wife or drink too much, but who also enriches the wealthy by slashing assistance programs for the poor, endorses capital punishment, and justifies a war with deceptive information. Much to the rest of the world's continuing amazement, we are still Puritans at heart.

In fact, many Christians believe that the sum of faithfulness is personal moral purity. Don't swear, don't dance, keep your nose clean, and don't consort with the wrong sort of people. How different this is from Jesus' teaching on purity.

Jesus lived in a culture where purity was a high priority. The Jewish system of purity laws defined one's righteousness before God in terms of keeping oneself pure from polluting influences. Certain foods (or combinations of foods) were to be avoided, women were separated from community during their menstrual cycles, and laws regulated the sort of contact with Gentiles which would be permitted if one was to remain ritually "pure." In many ways, these laws were grounded in good sense and healthy living, such as those regulating kosher foods. But the regulations of good sense tend to give way to rigidity over time, and by Jesus' day, this was the case.

Pharisees were the target of Jesus' criticism in this regard, and they make an easy literary foil for the good guys in the New Testament. They are represented as legalistic and hypocritical perfectionists. They tied heavy burdens around others' necks but didn't even observe what they themselves taught; they were fussy about the details of the law but didn't care about the weightier matters of love and justice; they excluded people and justified it by their religion.

But in fact, Jesus might have reserved his wrath especially for the Pharisees because their outlook was so similar to his own. So close and yet so far away. They may be caricatured as legalistic pea-brains in the New Testament, but the Pharisees were actually a religious movement that characterized what we might call today a "spirituality of the ordinary."

They brought the system of sacrificial ritualism and moral codes into everyday life. Certain prayers were said upon rising, washing, eating, working, and going to bed. They sought to sanctify the present moment, to use another modern term. The problem is that their attendance to the mechanics of this everyday spirituality led inevitably toward scrupulosity. Obsessed about the discipline, they forgot about the purpose of all this prayerful attention to detail. They strained a gnat (following the letter of the law) but swallowed a camel (ignoring the spirit of it all). Jesus was angry with them because like them, he cared about a spirituality of the ordinary; but unlike them, he didn't turn it into petty legalism.

So in response, Jesus proclaimed a different kind of purity. It was a purity of the heart. He cared about the law (especially in Matthew, from which the quotations below are drawn), but he asked his followers to go to the purpose of the law and not get stuck on the mechanics of it. In the fifth chapter of Matthew, Jesus asked for a transformation of the heart, not mere obedience of the lips and the body.

> Do not think that I have come to abolish the law or the prophets; I have come not to abolish but to fulfill. . . . For I tell you, unless your righteousness exceeds that of the scribes and Pharisees, you will never enter the kingdom of heaven. (Matthew 5:17, 20)

> You have heard that it was said to those of ancient times, "You shall not murder"; and "whoever murders shall be liable to judgment." But I say to you that if you are angry with a brother or sister, you will be liable to judgment; and if you insult a brother or sister, you will be liable to the council; and if you say, "You fool," you will be liable to the hell of fire. (Matthew 5:21–22)

> You have heard that it was said, "You shall not commit adultery." But I say to you that everyone who looks at a woman with lust has already committed adultery with her in his heart. (Matthew 5:27–28)

> And later in Matthew, he says:
> Are you also still without understanding? Do you not see that whatever goes into the mouth enters the stomach, and goes out into the sewer? But what comes out of the mouth proceeds from the heart, and this is what defiles. For out of the heart come evil intentions, murder, adultery, fornication, theft, false witness, slander. These are what defile a person, but to eat with unwashed hands does not defile. (Matthew 15:16–20)

The issue for Jesus was honesty. All of us get angry, all of us feel lust. He was not asking for an even more scrupulous Puritanism, one that controlled even our involuntary thoughts and feelings. He was pointing out that there is a continuum from irritation that runs all the way, eventually, to murder; there is a continuum that goes from a dirty mind to adultery.

Now obviously, some points along the continuum are more harmful than others. Gossip is not as bad as war, and taking delight in the beauty of a movie actress is not the same thing as pornography and promiscuity. However, Jesus' purpose in linking both ends of the continuum was to say, in effect, two things. First, no one is off the continuum entirely; no one can self-righteously justify themselves as "pure" and therefore be in a position to condemn and exclude those who are "impure."

Second, if we want to deal with the root cause of such forces as hatred, violence, abuse, and other evils, we must look into our own hearts. If we want to heal the world of its destructive energies, we must deal with the source of them within our own souls. This kind of spiritual work leads toward what Jesus meant by purity of heart.

Again, this does not mean that we become obsessive not just about our behavior, but also about our thoughts and emotions. It means that we become more aware, more honest about what is going on in our heads and hearts. Years ago, when I began practicing a form of meditation that required me to notice the nature of involuntary thoughts that arose in the silence, I was shocked at how much mental energy I consumed with imagining disaster, planning how I would get what I wanted, or worrying about what others thought of me. By coming to awareness about the actual state of our minds and hearts, we come to realize just how often we resent and judge others, how frequently we concern ourselves with our own needs and desires, how much worry and fear we carry around all the time.

What do we do with this awareness? Rather than using it as yet more evidence that proves us guilty of worthlessness, we are to become humble, more human. Accepting impurity of heart as a given of our human condition, we hold it before God in honest self-offering: Here I am, as I am. Take me as I am, transform me so that I become the person you intend me to be, and then use me for your purposes.

When we do this, we not only step out of the trap of behavioral scrupulosity and condemnation of others. We also step out of the trap of self-condemnation. No longer concerned about whether we or others measure up to external purity codes, we are free to see the light and the darkness as they are in our hearts, a sometimes bewildering and yet wondrous mixture of purity and impurity. Seeing this, knowing we cannot make ourselves completely pure, we then offer ourselves to God and depend upon divine grace to mature us spiritually and morally, from the inside out.

When we bring awareness to our heart and mind, when we see ourselves as we are—without shame or self-righteousness—and then when we depend upon grace to transform us, we are moved toward greater spiritual wholeness. This is difficult, but it is very important spiritual work. For the stakes are high. Without humble self-awareness, we stumble around blindly in the dark, causing great harm to ourselves and others. As Jesus said:

> The eye is the lamp of the body. So, if your eye is healthy, your whole body will be full of light; but if your eye is unhealthy, your whole body will be full of darkness. (Matthew 6:22–23)

Purity of heart can be given only by God, and it will never be complete in us during this lifetime. We are human, after all. But we can move, by God's grace, into greater purity of heart. We can, through self-awareness and surrender, expose and thereby weaken the impurities of our heart that plague us: our anger, anxiety, envy, malice, addictions, self-loathing, and fear. When I exposed the painful reality of my imagination and worries in meditation, I found that their persistence began to fade. Shedding light on my shadowy fears about disaster or plans to get what I wanted, it was as if they withered up under the light of truth. We can, through self-awareness and surrender, be healed and made new, so that we become more free to live the kind of life God intends for us to live: with a clear mind, in joy, equanimity, and compassion for others. We can, through self-awareness and surrender, experience something of what Jesus meant when he said:

> Blessed are the pure in heart, for they will see God. (Matthew 5:8)

drop your pride and shame

One day, Jesus told a story about a son who took his inheritance to a far-off land and wasted it in dissipated living. Coming to himself, he saw what he had become: a swine-keeper (not only a lowly job, but a forbidden one for a Jew). In shame, he imagined that if he could swallow his pride and return, surely his father would at least give him a place in the household as a servant. Instead, his father welcomed him home with outrageous abandon, scandalizing the older brother, who had remained at home all along, ever the good son.

The story of the prodigal son (Luke 15:11–32) is one of the best-known and most beloved parables of the gospel. It is represented in countless works of art and music. The story is so human, so real, so familiar. For every family either has a prodigal son or daughter who has returned to sanity and family life, or one who they wish would do so.

The story represents the outrageous way in which Jesus lived, and why he was so controversial: generous love for the outcast, the undeserving, and morally bankrupt; an open-armed embrace for anyone who turns to God in their hearts, regardless of their past; a feast of God's love that says no questions asked, amnesty for all, the important thing is that you were lost and now are found; you were dead and are now alive.

We identify with the prodigal son, and rightly so. The Father in this story is God, who always loves us completely, who always accepts us home when we return from our wanderings. But in identifying only with the prodigal, we forget that this is a story of two sons. In fact, it begins with these words: "Jesus said, 'There was a man who had two sons.'" (v. 11) The first half of the story is the familiar part, which concerns the younger son.

However, equal time is given, in the second half of the parable, to the older son. How many of us, when we think of this story, think first of identifying with the older son and his predicament? The church's historic emphasis on the younger son has not helped. After all, the parable has come to be known as *The Prodigal Son*, not as *The Two Sons*.

So one brother needs to be forgiven, and the other needs to forgive. We all need to learn how to accept God's forgiveness. We also need to learn how to forgive others. We are the younger son, and we are also the older son.

The younger son drew his inheritance early, went to a distant country, and squandered it all in dissolute living. He hit bottom. When he came to himself, he faced reality, squared his shoulders, and went home, repentant, intending to work as a servant so that he could earn back his place in the family. But before he could confess his shame, his Father was filled with compassion, ran to him, and welcomed him home with a feast. The Father didn't care about the past anymore; he was overjoyed just to have him back again. There would be no servanthood, no earning of love. All was freely forgiven.

Like the younger son, we wander far in a land where we throw away our potential, our inheritance. We are children of God, and yet we waste our loyalty on anxious overwork, material comforts, escapism. We are baptized into Christ, and we may listen to his gospel regularly in church, and yet we act as if we had never heard it, withholding our love, serving ourselves alone. Some of us have acted in ways that have dramatically wounded others. Some of us feel that we have cut ourselves off from God.

Like the younger son, at times we come to ourselves. We see ourselves as we are, and we make a vow to set things right again. We try to be nicer, we resolve to turn away from our idols, we announce our intention to be more spiritual, we fervently vow that this time, we really will become a better person. We make promises to loved ones that we won't work so hard or drink so much; we tell the kids that next year we'll be there for more of their games or concerts. Like the younger son, we say, "Father, I am no longer worthy to be called your child; treat me as a hired hand, just tell me what to do."

Without realizing what we are doing, we act out of the conviction that we must earn our way back into our inheritance as a child of God. We believe that we must prove ourselves worthy of God's love, that the only way to become more Christly is to work for it. But consider what happened when the younger son presented himself this way to the Father. The Father ran to him, wrapped his arms around him and kissed him, just overjoyed that he was no longer lost, no longer dead. Let the party begin.

In this parable, Jesus tells us that when we find that we have wandered far in a land that is waste, the only thing necessary is that we look in the mirror, come to ourselves, and open our hearts to God. The only thing necessary is that we return. We don't have to first clean ourselves up, fix all that we have broken, and present ourselves as certifiably worthy. We just have to come to ourselves and go home. God will rejoice and then do whatever is necessary to help us grow from that point on.

How did we, as a church, get to the point where we became a society for proper citizens, all cleaned up, sure of our moral superiority? After all, Jesus' community of prodigal misfits that he gathered around him included women with bad reputations, men with hardened hearts, and broken-down sinners like you and me, who all found themselves accepted and loved for the first time in their life.

Jesus offered love freely; it didn't have to be earned. His followers had only to look in the mirror, know how much they wanted this love, and come home to God. They regained their pride as children of God, because first they were treated that way by Jesus. To take the parable of The Two Sons seriously, to take Jesus' life and message seriously, we must stop believing that we and everyone else must earn our way back into God's good graces. We must simply come to ourselves, drop our shame, and go gratefully home to an overjoyed God who lays out a feast of love for us to share.

Then there is the older son. He is the one who doesn't need forgiveness himself. He needs to learn how to forgive. And in order to forgive, he needs to learn how to drop his pride. Upon the return of his brother, whom he spitefully refers to his father as "that son of yours," he unleashes a torrent of resentment. To paraphrase: "All these years I've worked like an obedient slave for you, and you never gave me the party I earned; but when this loser comes back, you drop everything and have a party."

It was clearly an unfair situation. Can't you relate? Imagine if your brother took off with precious family furniture or musical instruments, lost them all in a poker game, crawled home in disgrace in the hope that the family would put him to work in the family business, and was met by your father with a big party and joyful tears of relief! Maybe if his younger brother had first groveled for a suitable period of time, maybe if the Father had said to the younger son, upon his return, "Didn't I tell you so?" Maybe if the prodigal had been properly punished . . . after all, wasn't the Father just rewarding the bad behavior of the younger brother, even while he refused to reward the good behavior of the older one?

Like the older son, we believe that if we are good, God will then love us and bless us; if we aren't good, God will not love and bless us. We also believe that not only must *we* earn our way into God's love, so must everyone else. We expect fairness, which isn't all bad. People who do good should be appreciated, and those who do bad should be held accountable. But appreciation or accountability is not really the issue here. Unconditional love is the issue. Forgiveness is the issue. Openhearted acceptance is the issue.

The Father no doubt had a little talk with Junior the morning after the party. I would imagine that the Father held him accountable. But he never withdrew his love. He didn't withhold his forgiveness until the son could prove himself worthy of it. He simply loved, accepted, forgave, and celebrated. *Then* he held him accountable, I suspect. The Father also never loved the older son *because* he was good. He simply loved him, and had always loved him, whether or not he was good.

The two brothers in this story remind us both to let go of what we think we deserve, and also to let go of what we think the other deserves. God's love cannot be earned. It just is. Jesus told another story to illustrate this principle. Some workers came to work in a field first thing in the morning, some later, and some at the end of the day. All were paid the same. Where's the fairness in that, we may ask? But who do we think we are to question God's generosity? For as Jesus said, God "makes his sun rise on the evil and on the good, and sends rain on the righteous and on the unrighteous" (Matthew 5:45).

What we all deserve, in fact, is compassion and mercy. What we all deserve is what Jesus offered: welcoming one another into fellowship, forgetting the past, not holding onto resentments, and seeing one another as fellow sinners, fellow beloved children of God. We cannot earn God's love, and we should not expect others to have to earn ours.

This is very difficult to do, especially when someone who has hurt us continues to do so. In this case, we tend to stand on our moral high ground, refusing to come back down until the other admits he has been bad. Now to be sure, when another continues to do us harm, it is healthy for us to protect ourselves from further harm; but with God's help, we may still have an open heart of love toward them. We can keep internal boundaries that keep us from being too vulnerable, and yet also regard the other with care and respect. Then, when we step out of our self-imposed prison of bitterness and isolation, we can join the party that God wants to give for us all, even for our enemies.

In the end, the story of the two brothers is about the uselessness of both pride and shame, and the unconditional love of God. The younger brother was ashamed of his failure, but discovered in the love of the father that his shame had been a waste of time and energy. His father never expected him to crawl up out of his shame and earn his way back into favor. And while the older brother was proud of his rectitude, he discovered that his father had no use for it. The imagined necessity of staying in his father's good graces was never, in fact, required. He loved him whether he was a good boy or not.

God's love just is. It rains on the righteous and the unrighteous alike. We don't have to be ashamed if we fail; we just need to pick ourselves up and work with God to improve our lives. Neither do we have any right to be proud of ourselves, to imagine ourselves "worthy" of God. So drop both your shame and your pride. They're both useless, and God always loves you the same anyway.

be earthy

J esus was a carpenter. He lived in a small town in a semi-rural area, working in his father's workshop. His friends worked fishing boats for a living. They lived outdoors much of the time. They ate food that was local, simple, and healthy. Jesus went to parties where they roasted meat over an open fire, drank wine, and danced. He probably didn't bathe too often, and certainly didn't have many clothes to choose from. He was earthy.

Being followers of Jesus, we're called to be earthy, too, but not necessarily like this. One can be just as faithful a follower of Jesus in Manhattan as Montana. There are, however, qualities of earthiness that are universal for all who would follow Christ.

The word *human* is related to the words *humus* (organic and animal waste) and *humble*. To be truly human, therefore, is to be of the earth: an earthling, if you will. To be human is to be humble, to know that we are children of the earth and nothing more. As it says in the Ash Wednesday rite when ashes are placed upon our foreheads, "Remember you are dust, and to dust you shall return." At our graves, dirt is placed on the casket as the priest says, "Earth to earth, ashes to ashes, dust to dust." We are earth; we are made of minerals and water that come from Mother Earth. At our death, we return to the earth, out of which we arose. We are ashes, dust.

This is true humility: to know whereof we are made, what our limitations are, and our importance in the perspective of all of life. You are one of over 6 billion humans alive today. Think of how many more have already lived and will live in the future. You are a drop in the ocean. But we also know that we are—each of us—a beloved child of God, for "even the hairs of your head are all counted" (Matthew 10:30). So it is not that we are insignificant specks of dust; we are precious and beloved specks of dust!

This helps us put things in perspective. No matter what is going on in our lives, it probably isn't as big or as unique as we feel it is in the moment. We are also not as important as we sometimes like to imagine. In the face of the world population, in the face of eternity, the relative difference between the president of the United States and the homeless woman on the street is just not very great. We are all human, humus, humble, earthy.

Jesus understood this, and taught again and again about humility. Reserving most of his wrath for the Pharisees, he criticized them for their lack of humility. In the sixth chapter of Matthew, Jesus portrays them as ones who love to pray in public, so that they would be seen by others, who sound trumpets in the streets as they give alms, and who disfigure their faces when they fast so that all will admire their self-denial.

By contrast, Jesus' followers are to be humble, of the earth. They are to keep it simple, knowing who they are and who they are not. They are to give alms without even thinking about it ("do not let your left hand know what your right hand is doing," Matthew 6:3), let alone expecting a brass plaque with their names on it to be mounted in a conspicuous place. They are to pray in secret, quietly, in an intimate and humble dialogue with their Creator and not make a show of their piety. They are to fast without broadcasting what they are doing, without wearing ashes all day long on Ash Wednesday so that everyone knows they went to church.

And so in how we view ourselves, we are to remember that we are dust before God and before others. This means that we drop all pretensions about being super-religious or spiritually advanced. Spiritual pretension is not limited to Pharisees or to pietistic church-goers. In Zen Buddhism, there are traditional ways of undermining all pretensions of enlightenment. In some places, the Zen master is the only one who gets to take out the garbage. An easy, pious answer to the teacher's question is met with an outrageous action, such as a slap in the face or a word of nonsense. They speak of "the stink of Zen" (registering disgust at the pietistic words and actions of those who have become precious about their practice). There is a stink of spirituality, too, nowadays, as we wax nostalgic about our "experience of God." Remember you are dust, humus, human, humble.

In relation to others also, Jesus teaches us that we are to be earthy, humble. This is not about self-abasement and victimhood. It is about knowing that we are no better or worse than anyone else, and never in a position to judge others. "Do not judge, and you will not be judged; do not condemn, and you will not be condemned" (Luke 6:37). We are all fellow children of God, all highly valued and all of the earth.

Jesus lived with a wonderful combination of self-worth and humility. Without pride, he obviously held his head high and presented a strong self-image. Without any sense of shame, he knew how to blend into the crowd, never drawing attention to himself. He called his disciples to the same humility:

> When he noticed how the guests chose the places of honor, he told them a parable. "When you are invited by someone to a wedding banquet, do not sit down at the place of honor, in case someone more distinguished than you has been invited by your host; and the host who invited both of you may come and say to you, 'Give this person your place,' and then in disgrace you would start

to take the lowest place. But when you are invited, go and sit down at the lowest place, so that when your host comes, he may say to you, 'Friend, move up higher'; then you will be honored in the presence of all who sit at the table with you. For all who exalt themselves will be humbled, and those who humble themselves will be exalted. (Luke 14:7–11)

Remembering that we are dust, we are more likely to exhibit simple kindness to others. We are more likely to let others have the best seat, the best portion, the benefit of the doubt, the treatment we would like them to show to us. After all, we're all in the same boat.

Some of us, as followers of Jesus, are manual laborers, and some of us wear suits and ties to work. Some of us live in shacks, and some of us in mansions. Some appear on the society page, and some in the crime register. But regardless of our station in life, we are all called to humility. In the end, we all die and our bodies return to the earth and our souls to God. In eternity, we are all equal. This perspective helps us to remember who we are: precious but tiny specks.

associate with the wrong sort of people

Imagine the scene. A nice home, an elegant dinner. Soft jazz music in the background, salmon and California white wines on the table. Small talk about politics, children in college and lovely yoga retreats on the beach in Mexico. These respectable professionals and business leaders had invited an intriguing and disturbing young spiritual teacher who had begun to attract quite a local following. They greeted him coolly into the home, waiting for the right moment to set the intellectual trap that would expose him as a fraud, as someone they could dismiss.

Before dinner, servants brought in tasty tidbits to munch on, as they made small talk and gossip. But then, something shocking took place. A woman intruded. It was bad enough that an uninvited person interrupted this genteel gathering. Even worse, this was a woman who was known to be a sinner. Apparently everyone in the room thought they knew what her sin was, for she was already an object of gossip. Excluded from polite community, she was clearly not one of them.

And then, this party-crashing low-life gets down on the floor next to the young teacher and begins to cry—how embarrassing—and much to their horror, washes his dirty feet with her tears, dries them with her long dark hair, and then rubs them with a perfume that was even more expensive than that worn by the invited guests. It was outrageous, unacceptable. The host scornfully murmured, "If this man were an authentic spiritual teacher, he would know what kind of woman this is and would not allow her to touch him!"

But the young man speaks of her love, her tenderness. He points out that his hosts have treated him coolly, arrogantly; they didn't greet him with a kiss, or wash his feet, as she did. She is the one, this sinner, who has demonstrated real holiness, through her tender love. Then he does the unimaginable. Even though unauthorized to do so, he has the audacity to say that whatever she has done to incur their scorn, she is now forgiven.

Well, this was way over the top. We don't know what a dinner like this would be like after this bizarre encounter, but we can imagine might have been a little testy, to put it mildly. There aren't too many stories that appear in all four gospels, as this one does, in slightly different forms (Mark 14, Matthew 26, Luke 7, John 12). Why this one? Because it was emblematic of one of the central teachings of the early church. This story said something very important about what it meant to be a Christian, to be a part of the young Christian community.

After the example of Jesus himself, all kinds of people were being welcomed into the early Christian community, regardless of their social standing, their nefarious past, or even whether they were ritually pure according to religious law. Slaves, prostitutes, Roman soldiers, those physically handicapped, those demon-possessed, Gentiles, Greeks, Jews, women, children, rich, poor, everyone was included. In a highly stratified society, this was very unusual. Those who were excluded from proper religious society were especially welcome. As the outcast were brought again into fellowship with others, the terrible sentence of isolation from community was undone. This was unheard of.

Jesus got himself into trouble constantly over this, not just that one night at the house of the Pharisees. He invited himself to dinner at the house of a tax collector (who was hated by his fellow Jews as a collaborator with the occupying Roman army). He spoke directly to women, at a time when this was not proper for a rabbi. He probably shocked his own disciples when he healed the servant of a centurion. He included zealots (radical revolutionaries) among his disciples. Gentiles were welcome at his table and were healed by Jesus' touch, even though a practicing Jew was supposed to keep a physical distance from them.

Jesus could care less how this all appeared. He was simply not concerned about how his reputation might be called into question and his mission thereby compromised. Jesus knew he had his critics: "The Son of Man has come eating and drinking, and you say, 'Look, a glutton and a drunkard, a friend of tax collectors and sinners!'" (Luke 7:34) He looked into the heart of the individual, and there he sought and found God. What mattered to him was not the appearance, the externals, but the state of the heart.

And yet, how have Christians typically responded to this part of Jesus' teaching? We have a long and sad legacy of ignoring it in favor of social segregation. Private pews lined the front rows of old churches, heated by charcoal foot warmers, paid for by the wealthy, while the poor sat apart, in the cold. Black churches are kept separate from white ones, even today. Churches were set up for domestic servants by their employers so that they would worship separately. Homeless, smelly worshipers are quietly ejected by strong ushers so they won't disturb the clean and orderly folk at prayer. Bikers, druggies, punks, gays, misfits and poor minorities: Aren't these the kind of people Jesus partied with? Yet they are considered unclean by good churchgoers, kept at a great distance and worthy only of condemnation.

In my tradition of the Episcopal Church, it is obvious that we have done fairly well with many forms of segregation, except for one. We have attended to women, gay and lesbian people, minorities, and ethnic diversity—as long as they are well-dressed and articulate. If there is any doubt about this being a reality in our churches (and in many other denominations as well), just notice how much attention is paid at coffee hour to a new, obviously "successful" family—a doctor and a real estate agent—as opposed to a single mother who works at Wal-Mart.

Overcoming class and other social barriers is very difficult. For it requires of us that we not only transcend powerful social prejudices and convictions about others. It also requires that we deal with our fears about *the Other*. The Other is always frightening to us, because he or she is unpredictable. Around them, we are not operating in a comfortable sphere of predictable behavior and conversation. We must be open to the other as they are, not as a reflection of our own values and preferences.

A friend of mine, a priest, has done a great deal of work with congregations whose members are predominantly of racial and ethnic minorities in our country. He is Scottish, with pink skin and a doctorate. I asked him how he did so well in the ministry he is engaged in. He said that he has learned how to listen. He knows that he is in a culture that is foreign to him, and he enters into it with open eyes and heart, appreciating the distinctions of language and expression, values and priorities. He does not impose himself upon parishioners, but blends in with their world, so that he can learn from them. He is not afraid of them, but rather, curious.

Jesus blended in with those whom others in his society believed were not only different, but wrong. He remained himself, to be sure, but he also felt comfortable sinking into the ambiance of any social gathering. He was not threatened; he was not afraid. He looked into the heart, to seek out what sort of person this really was, beneath the externals.

Being a follower of Jesus means that we associate with the "wrong" crowd. We are to make friends wherever we find an open heart and a desire for God, no matter what "sort" of person they are. We are to drop our judgments that are based upon social conformity and look into the heart of each individual. We are to move beyond our fear and listen to the other. What we often discover when we do so is a refreshing perspective that gives new life to our dusty old religiosity. We discover the spirit of Jesus alive again.

how to find
the way forward

a job change beckons or is forced upon us: What now? What is the best use of our gifts, and how should we balance practical needs with our dreams? How long should we wait to hold out for what we really want? We're in a very unhappy marriage: How much effort to rebuild trust and intimacy is "enough"? Should we stick it out for the kids' sake, or will our unhappiness harm them worse than divorce? We're wrestling with decisions about the care of elderly parents: How do we balance family responsibility with our own personal needs and boundaries? When, if ever, do we override what our parents want with what we believe will be good for them?

Sometimes the way forward is clear as a bell. More often, however, we seem to be faced with two somewhat unattractive alternatives, because neither is without flaw. Both have their merits and their drawbacks. We make a list of both, and the list evens out. No help there. We pray for God's guidance, and nothing seems to come back. No skywriting, no burning bush. What do we do?

It is easy enough to say "things will work out," or "you'll know what's right," or "God will show you the way." All of these statements may be true, but in the meantime, how do we actively search for the best way forward? Or to put it in more traditional terms, how do we know when something is God's will for us?

Jesus didn't offer any simple formula to answer these questions, and we should be wary of those who do. But through his teachings and actions he did show a way of going about discernment.

First, he told us to pray for help and guidance (see the eleventh chapter of Luke). We are to make our needs known to God. We are to knock on the door, insistently if necessary. We are to trust that just as we know how to respond to the needs of our children, so God will grant us what we need and give us guidance.

It is surprising how often we forget to pray about the questions that perplex us. Or if we pray about it once, we assume that further entreaty is redundant or presumptuous. We figure if God doesn't want to answer us, we shouldn't bug him.

How different this is from Jesus' image of prayer. He encouraged us to be passionate, persistent, like children who will not let their parents alone until they respond.

Sometimes I face storms in my work that I have no idea how to navigate: A staff member becomes ineffective, undermining others' work; a pastoral counseling session suddenly becomes confusing for me; I have to guide others toward a financial choice that will hurt someone either way it goes. When sailing through these unfamiliar waters, I try to pray every day for God's guidance. I don't demand an answer today. I just hold the need before God, coming back to that place of questioning, waiting, listening, trying to be patient. If I don't get an answer, then I return to this place again, day after day. Over time, my questioning changes, my listening improves, my ability to be present to God in this quandary grows.

In the Zen tradition, some students are given *koans* to practice in meditation. A koan is an intellectually impossible question, a paradox that can be comprehended only by intuition, not understood by rational thought. One of the classic questions, for instance, is "Without words, without silence, will you tell me the truth?" Sitting in meditation with this question, one moves beyond rational exploration, into a more direct, experiential encounter with the question.

Similarly, the big questions about which we seek guidance must be approached by something other than the intellect. And persistent prayer, which Jesus recommends, is one way to do that. We can go over and over the merits and faults of this or that possible decision ad nauseam, and never be able to settle the question by this means. With constant prayer, we simply live with the question. This is what the Zen koan practice is all about: living with the question. Holding the question before God, patiently, daily, our perspective eventually shifts and we see everything from a new point of view. The way before us becomes clear, a third alternative comes to us, or the question just ceases to matter anymore!

Second, Jesus taught us to know the tree by its fruits (see Luke 6:43–44, for example). We are to look at the fruits, the outcomes and consequences, the ways in which a particular option manifests itself. Does it lead toward the kinds of things Jesus taught and lived? Does it lead toward greater love, faith, hope, and peace? Does it lead toward a more harmonious life for all concerned? In the unfamiliar waters I sometimes navigate, I listen deeply and patiently until some way forward appears that will serve the highest good of the staff member, the counselee, the finances of the parish. Often this way is not the most comfortable way, but it becomes, after a period of listening deeply, the only way.

This is the discernment process advocated by the Jesuits, outlined by St. Ignatius of Loyola. One is to become sensitive to the states of mind and heart that are generated by this or that possibility. If one way forward tends to stir up things that are unhealthy or unsettling—such as anger, self-justification, gratification of ego, etc.—it is probably not of God. If it stirs up greater faith, hope, honesty, and other signs of the Spirit, it is probably of God.

We speak of this kind of sensitive knowing nowadays as

the work of intuition. We wrestle with something, and sometimes we come to a place of feeling "in our gut" what is right. We intuit the right way forward, realizing that one option really "feels" more true than the other, even though we may not be able to explain this feeling rationally. Of course, this is not an instant method, and it doesn't always work like this. But often enough, we can feel our way forward by listening intuitively, by waiting patiently until we know what we must do.

The criteria by which we judge whether or not something feels right should, for Christians, be shaped by the gospel. But this is not a matter of simply deciding upon a list of "Christian" criteria as the "right" ones. Instead, as we give ourselves to Jesus' path more and more, as we learn that it is, in fact, a path that brings us life, we will naturally associate the qualities of Jesus' life and teachings with what feels right for us. He will influence us through our intuition. I find that if I am patient and prayerful about discerning difficult decisions in my work, that I get to the point where I *know* what I must do or say in supervising staff, in counseling, in making financial decisions with others. The Spirit has settled the muddy waters, and the way before me is clear.

And so through our intuition, we judge the fruits of a tree. We look at a person whom we are considering hiring; we consider how to respond to someone with whom we are in conflict; we listen to our motivations in trying to push something forward with our family or in our workplace: In all these situations, we examine the fruit—that is, the quality of the thing being considered. Is it true to the spirit of Jesus? Is it true with what I feel in my gut to be real, to be life-giving?

The "best" fruit, of course, is love. Love is the bottom line. And so we must ask, Does this or that way forward promise some degree of greater love for all concerned? But in answering this question, we must be careful. For what we assume to be love may be nothing more than our conditioning. Being nice and avoiding conflict are not the same as love.

Allowing someone to trample aggressively over us or others simply because we don't want to hurt their feelings is not the same as love. Sometimes, loving means doing the very thing that makes us uncomfortable, or that creates the most conflict.

In the end, we will not always know what God's will is before we have to plunge forward. Sometimes we just have to assume that since we have not received any guidance from the Spirit, God has left it up to us. The wonderful thing about this is that even if we make a mistake, God will work with that just as much as if we had made the "right" decision. For there is no place that God is not active in our lives. There is no place that God is not working to bring good out of anything and everything. God will continue to love us even if we make a mistaken decision for all the wrong reasons.

Sometimes I imagine that spiritually, we are in a kind of environment where all roads eventually lead to heaven. Out of wisdom we may choose the straightest road forward, or out of ignorance or stubbornness we may choose the most indirect path possible. Very few get on the bus marked "Express." Most of us get on the one that should be marked "Strangely Detoured." But the wonderful thing is, if we miss the right bus, another one will come along shortly, not to worry. God never gives up on us. Did you take this wrong turn? Fine, then we'll get there this way instead!

In the fifteenth chapter of Luke, Jesus tells stories about the one lost sheep, the one lost coin, the lost son who strayed. But God never allowed any of them to be truly lost. There was always a way home.

So it is with us. We may be able to find our own way with persistent prayer or with our God-given intuition, or we may not know what to do. But even if we become lost in ourselves, we are never lost in God. There is always a way home, and God will keep nudging us along until we find it.

enjoy the feast

Why was it that Jesus, speaking to poor and humble audiences, spoke so often about feasts? Because everyone knows about parties. A party is a celebration of life, a way of gathering loved ones and friends to shower generosity upon one another: eating, dancing, confiding, drinking, teasing, singing, laughing. At a good party we bask, for at least an evening, in the goodness of this world. Everyone, even the poor, can find a way of creating such an evening.

In one parable, wedding guests were invited to come, without charge, and enjoy the table spread for them (Matthew 22). They refused, but the host (God, of course) was so determined to share his generosity with others that others were brought in off the streets to take the places of the invited guests. Jesus frequented religious festivals regularly. In the second chapter of the gospel of John, he performed his first miracle at a wedding banquet when he changed a lot of water into a lot of very good wine. Jesus was even maligned as a "glutton" and a "drunkard" (Luke 7:34).

And what he left behind for his followers as the primary tool for staying in touch with him was a feast of love, the Great Thanksgiving: bread and wine, body and blood. In all this and more, Jesus' message was this: God is generous, life is full of divine goodness, so come, eat, enjoy what is offered to you.

It is typical of our modern culture to commercialize and

materialize everything. So even the gospel metaphor of the feast has been twisted into a prosperity message. Mega-churches buy whole shopping malls and offer not only worship, but numerous consumer opportunities for their members: mugs, t-shirts, DVDs, and aerobics set to Christian pop music. Sleek preachers in designer suits with their bejeweled wives sit on golden thrones before television studio audiences, telling the gullible that if they believe, if they tithe, if they send in their money *right now*, God will reward them with health and wealth. After all, we are the "King's Kids," meant to live royally.

All of this is a far cry from the kind of feast Jesus had in mind. Jesus' feast of the kingdom was a celebration of healing, joy, inner peace and unmerited love for others. It was not about wealth. The feast that Jesus celebrated was ordinary, accessible to everyone, anytime: nature, kindness, the breath of the Spirit, a simple meal of bread and fish, dancing, touch, laughter and music. All this is accessible to us as well.

Anything by overuse can become abused; anything can become an idol, promising something ultimate when its real purpose is more humble. But the fearful rejection of it can be problematic, too. Without the feast, we become tight, self-righteous, dour.

Jesus was not a Puritan or a monkish ascetic. He was an earthy, Jewish man of the world. As his followers, we can afford to let loose once in awhile and celebrate the goodness of life. The occasional feast is a form of worship, if we really understand that God is the source of everything healthy that is joyful and free.

But the parable of the kingdom of heaven as a feast goes far beyond the occasional party. It points to a way of living that doesn't depend upon a group of people, music, alcohol, or good food in order to find joy. The feast of the kingdom is always at hand, right under our noses.

The afternoon's golden light sparkles through the green

leaves, and playful shadows dance on the wall. The soft wind brushes against our cheek. A cat stretches in the sun, and a stranger smiles. The sweetness of a banana fills our mouth, the warm earth meets our bare feet, a cricket chirps, the cool of the evening settles all around. We touch our loved ones, and marvel at the distinct personality of every individual.

This is the feast of every moment, every place.

Jesus was awake and open to this divine feast of the ordinary, which gave him an inner reservoir of peace, enabling him to love, to heal, and to offer clarified wisdom to others. When we, like him, are awake and open, we celebrate God's life by being. Like the trees which stand in silent and dignified witness to it all, we sometimes drop our thoughts and tasks and become a part of the whole, no more or less important than a spider crawling slowly across the floor. The celebration of this festival of life's goodness is not just a happy little moment that provides a fleeting sentiment. It heals us. Then we, in turn, are in a position to be a healing presence to others.

My wife and sons and I have the great privilege of going to a family place on an island in a lake in New Hampshire once every year or two. It takes me awhile to settle down from the busyness of my life, but when I do I find that I'm drawn to the edge of the water, again and again, in order to sit quietly and just soak it all in. Waves and wind, sky and forest, saturating my soul. Nothing to do, nowhere to go, just settling into a place where I can allow God and creation to work on me. Without any effort or accomplishment on my part, my inner life becomes re-ordered, realigned on its own with God, so that I am once again directly in touch with the joy of being alive. I'm healed. And then when I return to work, I'm more able to give to others out of God's goodness in the center of my being.

I'm very aware that not many have the luxury of such a place, but we all have opportunities to do the same centering, where we are nourished by God's goodness. We can sometimes take a day at home where we enjoy sabbath time, turning off the telephone and the computer and everything else, forgetting errands and obligations, just reading, gardening, or looking out the window instead. We can go out for a picnic, we can camp in the woods, we can put on some music and sing and dance around the house.

These ways of being present and fully alive are not luxuries though we might make them so. They are natural, and they are just as critical to our life as water, food, and sleep. Humans throughout the world—wise old people, peasant farmers and laborers and mothers and children—have always had this natural capacity to stop and watch a sunset, to take a slow walk through the forest, to linger over a dinner with family, to fall into worship, so that their hearts are realigned and filled again with the goodness of the holy.

It is just that in our modern industrialized and electronic world that we seem to be driven at a pace that ignores these opportunities to be fully alive. We're working longer hours and taking the job home with us. We're taking less of the vacation time allotted to us than we used to, and when we do go, we take our cell phones and laptops, staying in touch with the office. We're always consuming, being entertained, seemingly never done with anxious duty. We are like the invited guests who ignore the invitation to the wedding banquet, and we ignore this invitation many times each day.

And underneath all this, the Spirit is always quietly present, like a servant, waiting at the table of our hearts, with a feast laid out for us, waiting for us to turn and feed on the goodness of life itself, which is never far away, never difficult to find.

So be good to yourself. Turn, and eat and drink of life's goodness. This is the wisdom of the Jewish weekly Sabbath; it is the wisdom of vacations, retreats, a quiet time reading a book with our children, a leisurely meal outside with friends, and an intentionally slower and simpler life.

This is the simple wisdom of what the saints have called *recollection*, or the *interior glance*: a habit of stopping throughout the day, opening the heart, looking for the beautiful and the miraculous in the ordinary, giving thanks in the midst of life. Without this nourishment, life will kill us. It is killing us. But if we feed on the feast of God's goodness in ordinary life, we will have what Jesus called eternal life, a reservoir of joy and peace within, and something to give to others.

Why is this so hard for some of us? Why do we ignore the feast that is laid before us, and starve ourselves instead with activities that do not give us life? I think that it is because on a deep level we really believe that it is we ourselves who must make our lives good and meaningful. So we work at it, always seeking accomplishment, pleasure, effectiveness, entertainment. We believe that if we do these things, we will discover that elusive peace and happiness and self-worth that always seems to vanish in the mist ahead.

God asks us instead to just be, to stop and open up: to rely upon something other than ourselves to receive, to come to the table and be fed. God asks us to rely upon something intangible, something we cannot control, something beyond us, something much more good and wise and true than us—so that this divine something can have the room and the time to rise up within us. This takes trust; it means that we must allow ourselves to be dependent, to be nourished by something whose presence and effect upon us we cannot control or guarantee. The divine feast of the ordinary is not *our* feast, after all: It is God's. We are only the invited guests, trusting the host.

As we risk the trust, we discover that we are not disappointed. Like me, sitting on the dock before the water, we find that our souls are re-ordered and centered again, that something infinitely loving and good does live within us, just waiting for us to allow enough room so that it can, on its own power and by its own wisdom, rise up and bring us eternal life, the kingdom of heaven that is always at hand.

forgive others

few religious teachings stand out as characteristic of their own tradition as clearly as forgiveness does for Christianity. Our faith has been marked forever by the picture of Jesus hanging on a cross, tortured to death by those who misunderstood and falsely condemned him, offering as nearly his last words, "Father, forgive them; for they do not know what they are doing" (Luke 23:34). We know that one of his central teachings, found in the Beatitudes, is to "love your enemies, do good to those who hate you, bless those who curse you, pray for those who abuse you" (Luke 6:27–28).

Living with a history of oppression by Roman soldiers, Jesus nevertheless responded compassionately to an officer who pleaded with him to heal a servant (Luke 7:8); he even taught that when a person (presumably a Roman soldier, since they commonly did this) demanded that a poor peasant carry something for him, the person should carry it an extra mile, and if struck on one cheek, to offer the other one as well (Matthew 5:38–42).

Jesus was surrounded by the petty legalism of small-minded religious authorities, who not only were incapable of hearing his wisdom and seeing his beauty; they plotted to kill him. And yet he befriended some of them: Nicodemus, who had come to him vulnerably, by night, and Joseph of Arimathea.

And of course, Jesus spent much of his ministry forgiving

people on behalf of a merciful God. As part of a time and culture in which everyone believed that here was a relationship between physical or mental disease and sin, he released them with acceptance and love. Those who were cruelly separated from community by virtue of being possessed by demons, having committed adultery, or afflicted with leprosy were restored to fellowship by Jesus' compassionate forgiveness and healing.

Christians are taught to forgive at every turn. In almost every act of public worship, we say together, "Forgive us our trespasses, as we forgive those who trespass against us." Sermons, pastoral counseling, spiritual direction—even secular therapy—all lead us to take seriously the call to release old resentments. We are told that even if we don't feel a responsibility to God to do so, we must recognize that if we hold onto anger, it will destroy us.

But what do we mean when we speak of forgiveness? Those who are rightly critical of this Christian emphasis point to our naïve tendency to overlook wrongs done, to passively accept things that should never be accepted. We have a habit of making nice, even as we are boiling within. We know how harmful this can become. Smiling all the while, we continue to carry resentment inside. It then pops out in vicious little comments, we try to drown it with alcohol, or we become depressed. By our pleasant piety, we refuse to see the faults of others, thereby enabling them to become even more destructive to themselves and their communities. Choosing "kindness," we allow injustice to continue. Clearly this kind of forgiveness is not what Jesus had in mind.

The forgiveness that Jesus lived had a subversive quality to it. Take, for instance, his teaching about going the extra mile with the soldier's burden, or offering the other cheek. The kind of response that a Roman soldier would expect as normal from a lowly peasant in this situation would be frightened submission or resentful acquiescence. To be faced with a peasant who smiled at the abuser, asked him about his children back home, cheerfully suggesting that they walk further together, standing firm after being struck and inviting him to do it again—this kind of behavior would be outrageously in his face.

What would be the result of this behavior? It would have the effect of taking away the power of the abuser. It would turn the tables, so that the offender hopefully might see himself for the brute that he is. It would place the intended victim in control of the situation. Suddenly the rules of the game would change.

Years ago, my congregation decided to publicly invite and then welcome gay and lesbian Christians in a liturgical peace offering. Recognizing the abuse they had received at the hands of the Church, we asked for their forgiveness as we welcomed them into our community. We did this at a time when (and because) the authorities in our diocese were putting forth a very different message of moral judgment against homosexuals. For this public act, the diocesan authorities angrily and publicly punished us by withdrawing a low-interest construction loan for our new house of worship. Many in our community were outraged. We considered legal action to enforce the loan.

Instead, we decided after much prayer and discussion to drop our "rights" and walk forward and simply be the community God was calling us to be. Releasing our anger and our hurt, it is as if we found ourselves in a boxing ring, having received the first hard blow, and then we *just stepped out of the ring*. Refusing to fight, we walked forward into the light of what we felt God was calling us to be, living without fear. We forgave those who punished us.

This act generated tremendous power. New members flocked to us, our building was paid off in 3 years, and the mean-spiritedness of the authorities was evident to all. But more important, we found the strength to become the community we were called to be that we would never have found by fighting. Ever since then, our congregation has been free to be ourselves, living without shame or fear in the midst of what is, at times, a difficult environment. And when we have occasion to worship and minister alongside those who tried to hurt us, we treat them with the respect they deserve as fellow children of God, as fellow sinners, all of whom are forgiven.

Many Christians labor under the false impression that forgiveness is the act of making ourselves feel good about someone who has hurt us. Such forced sentiments have nothing to do with the kind of forgiveness Jesus lived. Instead, his way was to subvert the power of violence and evil by changing the rules of the game—by acting in freedom and with respect for the others and refusing to be dragged into the gutter in which they insisted upon fighting.

In his "trial" and death, we see this most clearly. Falsely accused of trumped-up charges, feared as a dangerous troublemaker, he was the victim of a terrible injustice. But he didn't play the victim. He didn't rail against his abusers, entering into an ever-escalating conflict with them. But neither did he meekly knuckle under, cowering in apprehension or resentment.

Jesus chose a third path. He stood proudly, without shame or fear, telling those who thought they had command over him that they had no such thing. Given the context of Roman power and brutality, it was an astonishing moment when he said, "You would have no power over me unless it had been given you from above" (John 19:11). He refused to give them any power. And then, when Jesus was crucified, he didn't beg that they would have mercy on him; instead, in the hearing of his tormentors, he asked God to have mercy on *them*. This too was an act of power, even on the cross.

Thus by stepping out of the ring of hatred and violence, by forgiving them, he unmasked their injustice and revealed it for what it was. This was a deeply subversive act. It not only exposed the evil of his accusers; it revealed the power of God's love. For evil cannot be overcome by evil; it must be conquered by love. The result of this action has been that millions of people, for two thousand years, have seen in the cross the power of returning hatred for love, evil for good. In Christ, we have all witnessed the turning of the tables, where right relationships can be restored by blessing those who curse us. Forgiveness heals.

In the lifetime of many of us, we have also witnessed the power of this path as it has been played out very publicly. In the civil rights movement of the 1950s and '60s, Martin Luther King Jr. embraced the path of nonviolent resistance. Learning from Gandhi, he took the teachings of his Savior so seriously, so *practically*, that his movement and his life became an object lesson in the power of forgiveness.

Obviously those who were engaged in the movement didn't simply sit back and act nicely toward their abusers. This false caricature of "forgiveness" was what African Americans had lived with for far too long. Instead, King and others stood up to injustice with love. Refusing to return violence for violence, they stood firm in the face of hatred. Refusing to become a part of the cycle of destruction, they were free. They knew their intrinsic worth and their God-given rights, and they simply lived as if they were already given to them. By engaging in civil disobedience, they refused to play their part in the game of oppression. They took on the power they knew was already theirs. They acted in strength, with love.

The result of this essentially Christian movement was that it transformed society as we knew it. The oppressors were exposed, and the good became obvious. Injustice was not defeated by force; it simply crumbled before the beauty of truth. The mighty were brought down from their thrones, the lowly were lifted up, the powerful became weak and the weak became strong.

Our occasions for hurt and forgiveness are usually much less dramatic. A friend or relative says something that wounds us. A colleague undermines us at work. Our spouse betrays our confidence. A child rebels against our authority. These daily offenses are hardly of the same magnitude as racial oppression or crucifixion. And yet the principle is the same, no matter what the severity of the sin against us. By responding to the meanness, self-centeredness, or thoughtlessness of another with respect and continuing kindness, we reveal their actions for what they are, we retain our freedom and power, and we transform the relationship into something new.

When another person hurts us, we will quite naturally feel angry at first. But the path of forgiveness doesn't end there. It calls us forward, past the anger, to a fork in the road. One way leads toward "getting even," punishment of the other, and self-justification. The other way leads to understanding, continuing respect, and freedom from the bondage of negativity. The first way will only perpetuate a cycle of harm. The second way heals.

To take the direction that leads to freedom and renewal, we must first walk through whatever emotions arise, not attempting to manipulate them prematurely toward some desired outcome. At the same time, we must keep moving forward to a place where we might eventually release ourself and the other from the captivity of violence.

Eventually, by God's grace, as we refuse to engage in the fight, we come to understand that not only must we refrain from actively harming the other; we must refrain from engaging in mental and emotional violence against them even within our own hearts. For Jesus taught that internal hatred was the same as murder, in principle (Matthew 5:21–22). If we harbor resentment, we are still captive to the law of violence. We must learn to step out of the fighting ring that is located in our own hearts, refusing to fight the other even in our imagination. This is the deepest form of nonviolence: to back away from our natural human tendency to blame, condemn, or punish another within the confines of our own hearts. Jesus said that you must "forgive your brother or sister from your heart" (Matthew 18:35).

As we consciously do this, as we practice the discipline of external and internal nonviolence, we learn to understand the other, not condemn them. We learn to believe that they are as they are because life has shaped them that way, not because they are just mean, wrong, or evil. We still hold them accountable for their actions, but we also learn to respect them as children of God, sinners like us, who are stumbling through life just as we are. We learn to give back love for hatred, a blessing for a curse, a prayer for abuse.

Why? Not simply because we should, or even because we think it will please God. We do this because it is the only thing that works. It is the only response that will transform the cycle of harm into a new thing. It is the only thing that will heal us and the other.

This is never easy. It is tempting to assume that while this kind of response to others might be possible in cases of minor infractions, it becomes impractical, even inhuman, to expect it of ourselves when the stakes get raised. And yet, there is the image of Jesus on the cross, forgiving his enemies. There are his words to Peter, who wanted to know just how many times he should forgive another, even "'seven times?' Jesus said to him, 'Not seven times, but, I tell you, seventy-seven times.'" (Matthew 18:21–22). In other words, forgive without end. Don't ever stop forgiving. Don't ever consider any situation, no matter how hard, exempt from the call eventually to forgive.

don't be a slave to money

One day Jesus was approached by someone who wanted him to settle a dispute with his brother about their inheritance. Dear old dad was probably not yet cold in the grave when this man began to worry about whether his brother might get more than his share. Jesus responded:

> Take care! Be on your guard against all kinds of greed; for one's life does not consist in the abundance of possessions. (Luke 12:15)

The man probably thought he was only asking Jesus (in the role of the advice-giving rabbi) to determine what was fair, so that he could get the money that was coming to him. But Jesus perceived what was going on in his heart, and warned him against being so greedy.

Jesus then told him a story about a rich man who was so preoccupied with money that he failed to enjoy his life until it was too late. He worked hard, saved his money, and stored up abundant crops in brand-new, larger barns, thinking "Now I'm set for life and I can finally relax." But God said to him, "You fool! This very night your life is being demanded of you. And the things you have prepared, whose will they be?" Jesus concludes, "So it is with those who store up treasures for themselves but are not rich toward God" (Luke 12:20–21).

It was then that Jesus launched into a speech about money and faith, telling his audience not to worry about their lives, their clothing or food or any of their possessions. To paraphrase: Life is more than food, and the body more than clothing. Consider the birds, the flowers in the field, how God cares for them. Surely, God will care for you as well. By worrying, you cannot add one minute to the span of your life (in fact, you'll subtract from its length). So do not be afraid. Give generously what you possess, "for where your treasure is, there your heart will be also" (see Luke 12:22–34).

So in this twelfth chapter of Luke, what does Jesus teach us about the spiritual nature of our relationship to money in our modern, consumer-driven world?

First, he tells us that we must be careful about becoming so obsessed with making money for the future that we forget that we have a present. Now, some folks have to work two jobs in order to put food on the table. But many of us work 50, 60, 70 hours a week simply because the demands are there, we want to be a success at everything we do, and this requires that we don't disappoint anyone's demands. Regardless of how unreasonable the expectations for our time and effort may be, we dutifully slave away, and frequently our only reward for this loss of our precious time is a possible raise next year. Meanwhile, our children are growing up and life is passing us by.

Worst of all, when we feverishly chase the mirage of our financial security, we take ourselves out of the beauty and goodness of everyday life, as if happiness always lies somewhere else, somewhere better, somewhere more beautiful and fun. We become restless, never satisfied. This is exactly what the marketers want; but it takes away our life. It takes away our capacity to be present to the most satisfying things in life: love, nature, and an enjoyment of the simple things. And before we know it, our life will be over, and we will have missed it entirely. As Jesus cautioned: Take care, don't be greedy, for this night your life could be demanded of you. Stop and enjoy it before you lose it. This is a spiritual issue.

Second, the gospel tells us that worry and fear about money is a waste of time. Of course, we should be concerned enough about money to find work when we're unemployed, and to provide for our basic necessities. Worry is natural when there isn't enough food to eat. But this is a far cry from lying awake at night fretting about juggling cable TV subscription fees, insurance premiums, the state of our investments, and the possibility that we'll not have "enough" in retirement!

Jesus says not to be afraid, for it will not add anything to your life. We, as humans made in the image of God, are even more precious than the flowers and other animals of the world; surely things will work out for us, just as they work out for birds of the air and lilies of the field. God will provide, if we apply ourselves with our God-given talents and motivation, if we seek help when we need it. The rest is nonsense, demonic noise in our heads. This is a spiritual issue.

Finally, Jesus tells us that if we give up our fear about money, we will be much more likely to live generously. What a contradiction this seems to be. For we think that if we worry enough, we can make things work out. Then and only then will we be in a position to be generous. This is what is called *scarcity thinking*, which only leads to more fear. Afraid that there won't be enough to go around, we hoard and hold tightly (like the rich old fool in Jesus' story) in the fantasy that some day it won't be like this. Someday we will be able to afford generosity of spirit. For now (which turns out to be forever), we must rein in any impulse to let go.

The gospel calls us to *abundance thinking*. Only by leaving behind our fear about not having enough, only by stepping out in faith and giving generously of our resources (with or without money), will our treasure and our heart be rooted in the abundance of God's goodness. Fear leads to scarcity-thinking, and scarcity leads to a small life. Trust leads to abundance-thinking, and abundance leads to generosity. This is a spiritual issue.

How much money and how many possessions are truly enough for you? Do you live in fear about money? Why? Do you trust that you will be alright financially, in fact, that you already have enough to live generously, abundantly? Are you free enough from the marketing all around you to be able to resist being a restless consumer? Can you enjoy the simple things in life without needing to acquire more things?

When we challenge our relationship to money, we discover a greater degree of freedom, love, and faith. Jesus understood this, and called his followers to bring their relationship with money right into the middle of their faith.

evolve beyond violence

J esus lived in a brutal time. Roman soldiers were well-known for their swift and decisive violence. Jewish revolutionary zealots slit the throats of unwary soldiers. Then there was the usual: robberies, beatings, and murder. The most extreme example of violence in Jesus' life is the one made so graphic in the 2004 movie *The Passion of the Christ*: his own crucifixion.

In the cross, Christians have always seen not only the violence done against Jesus, but how he responded to it. The drama of the crucifixion teaches us a lesson that has been, in many ways, world-changing. It is certainly life-changing for many.

When Jesus was crucified, he did something completely unexpected, going against the grain of what we normally believe to be reasonable and expected human behavior when confronted by violence. What Jesus did has been held up ever since as a model of transformation, changing sin and evil into love, forgiveness, and new life. For what Jesus did was to overcome evil not by force, but by love.

Some of us live in dangerous neighborhoods, where muggings are a daily occurrence, where rapes and fights take place regularly. But all of us live with the reality of emotional violence: gossip, slander, rumor, painting in the worst possible light those whom we scorn. It is easy to slip into the dark attraction of hatred, self-righteousness, and condemnation: "Why, how *could* they? I would never *imagine* doing such a thing!" We tend to respond to emotional violence with the expected thing—a strong defense—thinking it is our right and our duty to do so.

When Jesus' own time came, when his own life was threatened by evil, sin, injustice, misunderstanding, when his own life was required of him by the powers of this world, he did not do the expected thing. Instead of resisting, striking back, or defending himself, he lived out of this other kingdom of love, and continued in faithfulness to God by loving, healing, reconciling, praying for his enemies, doing good to those who threatened him, regardless of their sin, their evil, their lies, their injustice. They could do whatever they wanted. Jesus' job was to be faithful to God's kingdom of love.

Jesus walked into the injustice and violence of his last week in Jerusalem with his eyes wide open. He knew that in order to do the most good, in order not just to respond to the passing urgency of the moment, in order to change history, in fact, he would have to *not* play by the rules that the world uses when it comes to conflict. He would have to *not* do the expected, reasonable thing.

Instead, Jesus would have to respond to evil, violence, and sin by continuing to love, forgive, heal, gather, pray, reconcile, and sacrifice himself as a means to further all of this beyond his own life. He stepped out of the ring of conflict, sacrificed himself, and turned evil into good through love.

At the time of this writing, the United States is at war. We have been at war, off and on, for nearly a century. Perhaps by the time you read this we will be involved in yet another war. Violence also comes in more personal, emotional forms. When a doctor makes a human mistake, we sue; when a neighbor neglects to clean their yard, we call the city hall; when we disagree with a politician, we curse and write an angry letter to the editor.

My prayer is that we might evolve as a species to the point where we learn to live and die as Jesus did, where we are willing and able to respond to conflict and danger as Jesus did, by a renewed commitment to love, forgiveness, gathering, praying, reconciling, doing good to our enemies, and sacrificing ourselves if need be, so that our familial bond as children of God will be preserved and strengthened in love.

We must not dismiss this alternative when the stakes get high, when it gets dangerous and personal, when friends disappoint or betray us, when another gossips behind our back. This is precisely when it matters most to be faithful to Jesus' way. To dismiss this alternative path as naïve, impractical, pious idealism is to deny Jesus' own faithfulness when the stakes got very high, dangerous and personal for him. It is to deny the power of the cross. It is to deny God's own revealed truth. Can't we learn to embrace the cross as the only way forward that will finally turn us from evil, sin and death to goodness, love, and life, as the only way forward that will transform the human condition?

I don't pretend to know how or when we will evolve as a species to this kind of faithfulness. But I believe that it is God's will that we do so. I also know what comprises your and my work: It is to pray for the fulfillment of Jesus' crucifixion in our lives.

As those who tread the way of the cross, our work is to refuse to fight by the rules of the world: to respond to personal attacks with prayer instead of defensive counterattack; to remain silent when gossip and slander try to seduce us with their promise of satisfaction; to continue to respect as a child of God even those who misrepresent and publicly criticize us.

Love is the only force that will last forever. Love is the only power that will conquer hate and violence at last. And love will triumph, because God is love.

be religious

I am religious. Jesus was religious. In fact, he was "into organized religion" as a practicing Jew. Institutional religion is natural, even necessary for human beings. For whenever two or three people are gathered around some form of personal spirituality, religious organization must eventually develop. Whenever one generation wants to hand down its spiritual treasures to another, an institution has to be formed. Otherwise what is precious to one generation won't survive for the next.

The root for the word *religious* is *religare*, which means to fasten, to tie, to bind up. There is one kind of religious binding that is destructive. We can all think of plenty of examples where people's freedom has been bound up and tied down by those who want to retain control and power. The fruit of this kind of religion is duty, judgment, repression, guilt, and subjugation. Jesus had plenty to say about this kind of *religare*:

> [Beware of the scribes and the Pharisees, who] tie up heavy burdens, hard to bear, and lay them on the shoulders of others; but they themselves are unwilling to lift a finger to move them. . . . But woe to you, scribes and Pharisees, hypocrites! For you lock people out of the kingdom of heaven. For you do not go in yourselves, and when others are going in, you stop them. (Matthew 23:4,13)

But there is another kind of *religare*. This is the kind of tying together, fastening and binding up that was used (literally) in the book you hold in your hands. Without some means to hold these pages together, they would fall all over the floor in random order, rendering them confusing and useless.

Jesus knew about this kind of *religare*, too. His spirituality was bound together by the religion of his time and place. Throughout his life, Jesus kept the Jewish law, worshiped in the synagogue on the Sabbath, studied and used the scriptures, observed Passover, and taught others to do the same. He expected people to obey the mandates of their religious tradition through prayer, worship, study, self-examination, confession, charity, and justice. He was fully a part of the Jewish religious community. And at the end of his life, he was engaged in a celebration of the Passover when he instructed his disciples to celebrate a modified version of this ritual as a way of continuing to call upon his presence.

As humans, most of us need structure in order to function and flourish. That which is ultimately formless and beyond all comprehension—God—must, for us humans, be fastened together in some form so that we can lay hold of it. The various religions and spiritual traditions of the world are bound-together forms, employing practices, language, symbols, sacraments, scriptures, and rigorous means by which some are trained and authorized to teach the tradition. All of this provides a pathway that enables people to enter into the divine mystery, without which we would fumble around alone in the dark.

A religious life that is faithful to the spirit of Jesus is one that holds the tradition lightly, with plenty of room for individual interpretation and freedom of movement, with a high tolerance for criticism and doubt. This is, after all, the kind of atmosphere Jesus himself created around him.

A religious institution that has this quality of life will be like a large home where lots of people might choose to live.

This home has certain furnishings and symbols that inspire and delight its dwellers. It observes traditions of food, festivals, stories, and other customs. It has basic rules that create order. Guests are welcome and respected, even though they come from a different kind of home and tradition. Residents come and go, even traveling for extended periods to other religious environments, bringing back tokens of their experiences, which are put in places of honor in their home. But the home remains its own distinct environment. It is a kind of porous place, open to other ways, open to question and evolution, but it always retains the important elements that have shaped its identity. It is also a home where no subject is forbidden to bring up, to question, or to doubt. There is room in this home for skeptics.

Jesus was a man of his time, his culture, and his religious upbringing. He was critical of it, even though he loved it and never left it. He used it as an imperfect, limited, very human, external expression of something that is beyond all form, all limitation, all structure. He used religion as a "good enough" vehicle that could, at its best, transmit something of divine transcendence. But he also understood that religious structure and the living God are synonymous. Even though he used the religious form, he took it lightly; he was ultimately free of it. After all, God freely moves through life, and is not imprisoned in religion.

don't be too religious

a s the Zen tradition says, the finger pointing to the moon is not the moon. The map is not the territory. At some point in our use of religion, we realize that the form which leads us into formlessness is not God. Our religious practices, teachings, and traditions are only tools, and they are only *one set* of tools, standing alongside the tools of other traditions. The Bible is not God. The sacraments are not God. Even the doctrines and creeds of the church are not God. They are imprecise human expressions of the infinite mystery of God.

So here's a call to use religion lightly. It's just a form, not to be taken too seriously. We may enjoy its beauty, ponder its wisdom, and apply its guidance to our lives, but we must never mistake it for the thing itself, which is God.

When we make religion overly important, we fall into pietism, a kind of sentimentalized attachment to religious trappings. Or we angrily defend our position, insisting that there be no wiggle room for heretics to compromise the faith. We point the finger at others who fall short of our moral expectations. We become scrupulous about our practice, beating ourselves up for missing a time of prayer or Sunday worship, and we feel guilty for our lack of faith or failure to love.

And the tragedy of misplacing our attachment to God for an attachment to the form of religion is that we miss the boat. We replace a liberating relationship with the living God with mere pietism, scrupulosity, moralism, theological certainty, or perfectionism.

It is common these days, when trying to avoid being too religious, to embrace "personal spirituality" as the alternative. But it is also possible to take personal spirituality too seriously. For example, many today are both attracted to and frustrated by their attempts to use various spiritual disciplines: daily prayer, fasting, and so on. Spiritual discipline then becomes a kind of yardstick by which one grimly measures one's spiritual worth, rather than enjoyable means toward liberation and happiness. The effort to "be spiritual" then quite effectively distracts us from the real thing: living freely and spontaneously in God's presence. Instead of simply opening one's heart to the music of God in life, we find ourselves fussing around with the instruments of religion. One cannot only become too religious; one can be too spiritual as well.

The most shocking and powerful warning I have heard about this dynamic is one of the sayings attributed to Jesus in the Gospel of Thomas:*

> If you fast you will bring sin upon yourselves,
> and if you pray, you will be condemned,
> and if you give to charity, you will harm your spirits.
> (Gospel of Thomas, saying 14a)

What? I thought one was *supposed to* fast, pray, and give to charity! Didn't Jesus teach us to do these things? Aren't fasting, prayer, and almsgiving the pillars of Christian devotion, commended to our use especially during the season of Lent? Yes. However, when we become too religious, too self-consciously focused on the mechanics of spiritual practice, fasting brings sin, prayer brings condemnation, and charity damages us and others.

We sin when we fast if we replace an empty, open availability to life with mere abstention from food. In obedience to the mandate to withhold food from our bodies, we may assume that we've thereby fulfilled the whole point of fasting (which is to become empty and free), even if we haven't.

We are condemned when we pray if we substitute being animated from within by the divine energy that fills all creation for a dualistic "relationship" with a "being" who is impossibly "other." This kind of prayer may actually prevent a real opening to grace. In dutifully praying on a regular basis, we may assume that we've thereby fulfilled the point of prayer (which is to open ourselves to God's presence and action in our lives), even if we haven't.

We harm our spirits and the spirits of others when we give to charity because we have traded the act of generosity with real love and mercy. In stooping to help the other, we may feel better about ourselves, but in doing so we may separate ourselves from the other who is "not like us" and thereby damage the relationship.

Practices like these aren't always destructive, of course. But there is a way in which the disciplines of spirituality bind up the very thing it is supposed to liberate. There is a way in which spirituality can keep out God.

I have become much less interested in spirituality as I have become more interested in life. I know that all the years I spent carefully practicing disciplines of the faith were useful. They led me to the point where they became integrated enough so that I could either use them or ignore them, as the situation called for. Like training wheels, at some point they just fell off, and I began riding the bike itself, which is life in God.

Prayer is now more a way of just being open than it is a distinct activity. I still pray, in worship, intercession, petition, and meditation, but I don't make myself "practice" prayer and spirituality the way I used to. To do so has become a burden, an artificial activity that actually separates me from the thing that prayer and spirituality are supposed to lead us into.

Instead, I live with a more open heart, more fully engaged with life itself (which is infused with God), struggling with difficulties that life presents, wondering at beauty, feeling the frustrations and marvels of my humanity, doing the work that God gives me to do, handing over to God those things I need help with, enjoying quiet moments when they come, and slipping in and out of intentional forms of prayer and spirituality when the need arises.

The finger pointing to the moon is not the moon. The map is not the territory. Religion is just a form. While fingers and maps and religions may help us get oriented, once oriented we must then venture out into the territory itself.

*Many dismiss these and other early church writings that lie outside what was eventually established as the canonical New Testament as heretical. I see them as minority voices that were puzzling to the majority of other Christians, but which nonetheless express wisdom. They are akin to the minority contemplative tradition throughout the two millennia of church history, many of whose proponents have frequently been excluded from the mainstream, even tried as heretics. The Gospel of Thomas is a collection of enigmatic sayings, with no narrative explaining them or providing a dramatic flow. Standing starkly alone, these sayings work on those who ponder them like Zen koans, puzzling us at first, until they eventually unlock something for us that is deeply true. Certain early Christians wrote down and shared these sayings, using them to deepen their faith life. Many of them are identical, in fact, to the enigmatic sayings of Jesus found in the canonical gospels. But many others, like the one cited here, are quite unique. It is quoted from:

Marvin Meyer and Stephen Patterson, trans. "The Gospel of Thomas," *The Complete Gospels: Annotated Scholars Version*, Robert J. Miller, ed. (Santa Rosa, CA: Polebridge Press, 1994).

trust in Jesus

many spiritual seekers, genuine in their quest, cannot bring themselves to "believe in Jesus Christ" in the way that they think the church expects them to. Some grew up in a Christian tradition that demanded strict obedience to doctrine and moral teachings. As they matured, they discovered that life wasn't quite so black and white as it was presented to them. Perhaps they went through a divorce or came to know closely a gay or lesbian person. They became friends with Buddhists, Jews, Native Americans, Muslims, loving agnostics, none of whom seemed wicked enough to be consigned to hell.

All of these experiences began to undermine the rigidity of their religious upbringing, eventually rendering it less credible. Now when they hear Jesus referred to in the Nicene Creed as "the only Son of God" or the admonition in John 14:6 that "No one comes to the Father except through me," they can't buy it. Christianity and the teachings of Jesus then become inaccessible for them.

Others have never worried too much about these things, being more comfortable with theological ambiguity and the ultimate love of God for all people. For them "belief in Christ" is the way that Christians enter more deeply into their faith life, just as people of other traditions place their belief in other things. And yet they, too, sometimes squirm when they hear the exclusive language voiced by televangelists or even in the

traditional phrases of their own scriptures, creeds, and liturgical prayers.

An analysis of the doctrines of the church lies outside the
scope of this book. And yet, if we are to take to heart the
teachings of Jesus, we must deal at least briefly with this question of "belief in" him.

There are plenty of New Testament passages that call for
belief in Christ. Primarily found in the letters of Paul and in
the gospel of John, these texts were written by members of
the early church as statements of their faith experience rather
than factual reports of historical events. Even the gospel of
John should not be understood as direct quotations of Jesus
and a historical record of his actions, but rather as a portrayal
of how the Christian community experienced the risen Christ
in their faith and worship. In their writing of the gospels, they
were proclaiming their spiritual experience of Christ.

And so the passages in John that refer to belief in Christ
should be heard as "Jesus is for us the way to God, the truth
and the life; he is our light, he is our bread, our gate, our true
vine" (see John 14:6; 9:5; 6:48; 10:9; 15:1). This brings a very
different feel to the texts than if Jesus were pointing to himself, saying, "I am the way, the only way, for everyone without
exception."

With this in mind, we can read the gospel of John and the
letters of Paul, both texts that emphasize the necessity of belief in Christ, as faith statements of certain leaders of the
early church. But even this should not be seen in an exclusive
way. Reading the whole context of these writings, one sees
that they did not demand belief in Christ in order to condemn
everyone who did not share these beliefs. They did not have
in mind all the Jews, Buddhists, Muslims, Hindus, agnostics,
and native people of this world, thinking, "Well, they may be
decent enough people, but they're all going to hell for eternity if they don't become baptized and believe these theological propositions about Jesus Christ."

Instead, I think that their effusive (and sometimes exclusive) language was the language of love. They had encountered the spirit of the resurrected Jesus, and it had changed their lives. They wanted nothing more than to share this wonderful, liberating experience with the whole world: Jews, Greeks, atheists, everyone. The wonderful news was that now one didn't have to live up to religious laws and rules in order to earn one's way into heaven; instead, one could find freedom through a relationship with the living spirit of Christ, as they had. It was more a free offer of food from one beggar to another than a set of rigid beliefs that fenced off heaven from hell.

Effusive, even exclusive language was the way they expressed their enthusiastic desire to share what they had found. After all, when one falls in love, one might say, "I met the most wonderful, beautiful woman in the world," never meaning to imply that there are no other beautiful women on the planet. Similarly, certain members of the early church said, in the enthusiasm of love and liberation, "This Jesus is the way to God! He has changed my life! You, too, can drink of this living water!" It is the *good news* (translated as "gospel"), a positive message of what happens when one enters into a relationship with the living Christ. It is not the bad news of what happens when one does not.

If one then turns to the synoptic gospels—Mark, Matthew and Luke—(the gospels that are more historically accurate in terms of Jesus' own teachings), one sees this good news even more clearly. In these three gospels, Jesus is not running around pointing to himself and demanding that everyone believe certain theological propositions about him. He points to "the Father," to whom all have a natural and equal access. He talks about life, love, faith, forgiveness, relationships, poverty, justice, and all the ways in which we might enter more deeply into an authentic and liberating life of faith. He asks people to follow him into this life of freedom that he knows and lives and passionately wants to share. He wants us break the chains that keep us imprisoned and to go with him, all of us together, into the kingdom of God.

And yet, over the centuries the church has at times still emphasized the exclusive message of condemnation. Why? Partly because this message controls the masses. If you can threaten people with hell, many of them will be more likely to obey you. It also has a way of strengthening one's own position, so that one might give oneself to it with more certainty and abandon. And in fairness to the early church, they wrote these scriptures and creeds and doctrines at a time when the very fragile, nascent Christian community was in the process of splitting into a hundred splinter groups, each with its own set of beliefs and customs. If this had continued, Christianity, and Jesus' liberating gospel with it, would have disappeared off the face of the earth. Certainty and theological boundaries had a way of helping the church survive.

What then does one do now with the church's directive to "believe in Jesus"? One approach is to toss it out entirely, but that has a way of constantly putting us at odds with the Bible and the church's worship, since in these places we are frequently confronted with that which we have rejected.

But there is another positive use of "belief in Christ" that is both faithful to the church's experience and teachings, and also nonexclusive. It is to understand that when we believe in something or someone, we place our trust there. When we really believe in our partner in love, we place our trust in them. We count on them to be there for us, to be true and faithful to us. We know that as we place our trust in another, they will come through. We will follow that person anywhere, because we believe in him or her.

The same is true with Jesus. When we place our trust in him, when we open our heart to his spirit, he comes through. He then lives in us, he teaches us by his presence, and he guides us into a free and vital life. Jesus is spiritually alive, after all. He is not just a revered dead teacher of the past. The

Christian community believes that he is spiritually alive as a resurrected presence, available to anyone who turns to him in faith. As we place our trust in this presence, he comes through. This is believing in Jesus, much more so than believing certain theological doctrines about him.

It is far more challenging and rewarding to place our trust in Jesus than merely to believe that doctrinal statements about him are objectively true. For what does it really mean to simply say, "I believe that Jesus died for my sins, that he is my savior, that he is the second person of the Trinity and the only way to God"? Perhaps nothing. Just because one believes that these things are true does not necessarily mean that one is any different, any more loving, any more connected to God than if one didn't believe these things.

By contrast, if you place your trust in Jesus, if you open your heart to his life-giving presence, you will enter into a relationship of faith that will change you. You may be more likely to try to forgive instead of holding onto resentment like a security blanket; you may look at that homeless person at the freeway on-ramp a little differently; you may start to awaken to the quiet joy of just being alive in God, even when things are not going so well for you. Like any relationship, you will be asked to risk the experiment of living as he lives. This relationship will make you, by your efforts and by the grace of God, a more healthy, loving, courageous, and faithful person. You will, in fact, become more like Jesus himself, taking on his own character.

This approach to belief has always been the real heart of the church's teaching about Jesus, not the threat of condemnation for those who are unorthodox in their theology. This teaching began when the members of the early church discovered that Jesus' spiritual presence liberated them and changed their world. And so they proclaimed, "If you, too, place your trust in him, he will do the same for you!"

When we trust in Jesus this way we begin to know, from

the inside out, what it means to follow him. He speaks to us from within, calling us to live generously, to let go of worry, to turn from sin toward an always-loving God; we listen, we follow his bidding, and we are changed. When Jesus walked the region of Galilee and invited people to follow him, he was not just asking them to travel where he was headed down the road. He was not even just asking them to coolly and objectively consider his teachings, alongside the valid teachings of other spiritual masters. He was asking them to journey with him, to enter into his life, to experience what he had to offer. He was asking them to allow him some space in their heart, so that he could affect them in a personal and loving relationship. He was inviting them to place their trust in him.

When they did so, their following was something far more than mere theological certainty. Their following was a fully committed entrance into a way of life, with Jesus as their guide. As their belief gave them the ability to place their trust in him, their following allowed them to go with him where they might not otherwise be able to go. Jesus led them, as they trusted in him, into new spiritual territory.

So it is with all who trust in and follow Jesus. We, too, are attracted to his teaching, to his refreshing and authentic character. He catches our attention and his words penetrate deeply into our souls. If our response to Jesus remains cool, detached, and objective, we might benefit from him as we would benefit from any wise teacher. But if we know in our heart that his words, his actions, and his character are deeply and authentically *true*, we will be drawn to place our trust in him. We will enter into a relationship with him. We will begin to count on his presence and his guidance as he leads us into the kingdom, and we will follow him into its depths. We will then know for ourselves the good news that the church has always proclaimed: "you shall know the truth, and the truth will make you free" (John 8:32).

pray for what you need

Those of us who like to think of ourselves as religiously mature tend to avoid praying for what we want and what we need. We are "beyond" that spiritually, because we see how this can be so self-serving: O Lord, I've been faithful to you, and now I need you to bless me with that cushy job I've applied for—I'll tithe, I promise! O Lord, make Susan nicer, help her to see the error of her ways.

Or maybe we avoid praying for our own needs because we know that we shouldn't even be concerned about ourselves; we should always be other-centered. So we pray diligently for other people, asking God to heal, bless, and assist those in need, but never for ourselves. Perhaps we just sit in contemplative silence, never asking for anything, because we know that God already knows our needs before we ask.

As a reality check, let's return again to the one prayer that Jesus taught his disciples when they asked him how to pray: Give us this day our daily bread. Forgive us our sins. Save us from temptation, deliver us from evil (see Matthew 6:9–13). These are real needs. In the plural voice, they pray not only for others, but for ourselves as well: give *us*, forgive *us*, save and deliver *us*. We all know just how concrete these needs really become. Hunger, sin, temptation, evil. These are real.

Throughout his ministry, Jesus prayed for concrete situations, with passion and desire. Jesus was grieved in his heart and wept with Martha and Mary over the death of their brother, his good friend Lazarus. He responded lovingly to a woman's passionate need for healing that drove her to just try to touch the hem of his garment as he passed through a crowd. Surrounded by grief-stricken relatives, he begged God to bring a little girl back to life again. He prayed that God would multiply bread and fish in order to feed a hungry crowd. And he didn't reserve his prayers only for others. In anguish, sweating blood, he pleaded that God would spare him from the crucifixion. These were real desires, real needs, and he prayed that God would respond with real action.

It is important that our desires come into our prayer, and that we not remain neutral, stoic, unconcerned about whether or not our needs will be met. Why? I believe it has to do with the powerful chemistry that happens when our passion joins together with God's passion. When we want and need something that is good, and God wants for us the same thing, and when those two desires come together, a kind of alchemy takes place that is very strong. It is like when two people fall in love; their passion for one another is a force of nature; it has a life of its own that is much more powerful than the desire of one person alone.

And so it is with our prayer. It is one thing for us to desire something, or for God to desire it for us. It is quite another thing for those two energies to come together. Our human will is a powerful thing. With it we can dam up vast river canyons, we can enslave millions of people, or we can push through immeasurable personal difficulties. God's will is an infinitely more powerful thing. With it the heavens and the earth were made, people's very lives are transformed, and entire nations have been motivated to rise up and claim their liberation. So when these two powerful forces come together, a new creation is potentially born.

As we pray for something concrete we pour the energy of our desire and our will into God's own desire and will. When there is a match, the world moves. "Even if you say to this mountain, 'Be lifted up and thrown into the sea,' it will be done" (Matthew 21:21). When our will and deepest desire finally become aligned with God's will and deepest desire, amazing things happen. An alcoholic miraculously loses all desire for drink. A breakthrough comes in a marriage. Reconciliation happens between enemies. Childhood traumas are healed. A people rise up in nonviolent resistance in order to highlight the injustice of racism, and centuries of institutionalized bigotry are struck down. Mountains of all kinds are lifted up and thrown into the sea.

Jesus also taught us that in praying for our needs and the needs of others we are to do so with persistence. "Be demanding," he said! Jesus tells this parable:

> Suppose one of you has a friend, and you go to him at midnight and say to him, "Friend, lend me three loaves of bread; for a friend of mine has arrived, and I have nothing to set before him." And he answers from within, "Do not bother me; the door has already been locked and my children are with me in bed; I cannot get up and give you anything." I tell you, even though he will not get up and give him anything because he is his friend, at least because of his persistence he will get up and give him whatever he needs. (Luke 11:5–8)

We can just picture the scene. Perhaps you're in crisis with your spouse, you can't sleep, and a friend in the neighborhood is the only person you can talk to. So in the middle of the night, you go to her house and ring the doorbell. No response. You *have* to talk. You keep ringing and shouting, setting off barking dogs, waking up all the neighbors. What can your friend do? Finally she says, "Oh all *right*, I'm coming! What do you want?"

Jesus often told humorous stories that made his point in

extreme ways so we'd be sure to get the point. Obviously, God is not stubborn; this is not why we must be persistent in prayer. God is loving and responsive, but for reasons that we will never understand, does not always respond to our prayers immediately. And so what do we do? Perhaps we slink away, feeling defeated, less likely to pray for what we want the next time. But Jesus asks us to be persistent, like the friend at midnight, demanding a response from God. We are to keep praying until God responds. Why?

Persistence in prayer is necessary because what we are first asking for is not necessarily what we eventually need to ask for. For a long time, our motivations remain muddy and our intention unclear, and we must journey toward purity of heart. What is it we really need? What is it we really want? What is the right thing that will serve not just my own preferences but the higher good for all concerned? How is my desire for change complicated by self-serving interests? What am I unwilling to let go of or take on for real change to occur? How am I perpetuating the very thing that I seek to change?

These are questions we must slowly pick our way through before our desire and will become clarified. Persistence in prayer is needed not because God is hard of hearing, but because our prayer gradually has to evolve to the point of becoming pure. "Blessed are the pure in heart, for they will see God" (Matthew 5:8). Blessed are those whose desire and whose will have finally distilled to the point of clarity, for their pure intention shall be matched then with God's pure intention, and the two shall burst into a new creation.

Frequently, Jesus asked people (whose need was probably obvious to him), "What do you want me to do for you?" This was a way of getting them to be clear about their intention. In one healing story in the fifth chapter of John, a paralyzed man lies helplessly by the pool of Beth-zatha, whose waters contained healing properties. He has been there 38 years (and probably making a living as a beggar). Jesus perceives the situation, and asks, "Do you want to be made well?" It may seem like an obvious question, but perhaps this man really didn't want to be healed. In fact, he does not say, "Of course!" Instead, he complains, "Sir, I have no one to put me into the pool when the water is stirred up; and while I am making my way, someone else steps down ahead of me." His intention is unclear, and he has lost all sense of hope. Persistence is not possible for him at this point.

If we are persistent in prayer, and as our intention becomes more in tune with God's will, it is reasonable to expect that God will answer our prayer. According to Jesus it is natural to expect a loving response from an intimately loving *Abba*, Father:

> Ask, and it will be given you; search, and you will find; knock, and the door will be opened for you. For everyone who asks receives, and everyone who searches finds, and for everyone who knocks, the door will be opened. Is there anyone among you who, if your child asks for bread, will give a stone? Or if the child asks for a fish, will give a snake? If you then, who are evil, know how to give good gifts to your children, how much more will your Father in heaven give good things to those who ask him! (Matthew 7:7–11)

But what are we to make of the fact that our prayers are sometimes not answered? For even if we have done our very best to work slowly through the muddy waters of intention and come to a place of selfless desire, sometimes nothing happens. A child dies of cancer after the parents have spent months in truly selfless prayer and soul-searching. The deadness of depression returns again and again, even after years of faithful efforts to deal with it. Despite the earnest intercession of millions of peacemakers, we still go to war, killing thousands of innocent children, mothers, sisters, and brothers.

Most of us have heard Matthew 21:21–22 taken out of context and applied as a universal and immediate truth: "If you have faith and do not doubt . . . whatever you ask for in prayer with faith, you will receive." Endless effort has been wasted by those who try to rid themselves of any residue of doubt, so that the desired outcome will indeed come to pass. Applied to any and all situations, this notion becomes a way of instilling guilt: "I didn't get what I asked for; it is because I don't have enough faith." Taken this way, the "faith" of the believer becomes a magic wand—if held correctly and accompanied by the right words, "Abracadabra!" God takes action, like a genie released from a bottle!

I don't pretend to understand why sometimes God does not grant the good thing that a person selflessly asks for: healing, renewal, protection, peace. But I do know that God sometimes gives exactly what is asked for. And more important, I believe that God always gives something in response to a prayer that is persistent, selfless, and full of faith. What is given may not be what is asked, but something will be given. We are to pray with as pure an intention as we can come to, and then let go of the results.

Even Jesus had to do this. In the Garden of Gethsemane, during his lowest hour, his friends having gone to sleep in spite of Jesus' plea to remain awake with him, Jesus prayed in agony and pure desire, "Abba, Father, for you all things are possible; remove this cup from me; yet, not what I want, but what you want" (Mark 14:36). He expressed his need and deepest desire, and then let go of the results, surrendering everything into God's hands. What Jesus asked for was to be spared the crucifixion. God's response was not to circumvent the cross, but to bring him through it to resurrection. Jesus asked for one thing, unable to see beyond his immediate concern, but God saw further, and responded in a way that Jesus, in his humanity, could never have envisioned.

A number of years ago I was in need of a full-time assistant priest, and had hired a local person for an interim while we conducted a national search. After months of fruitless searching and what we thought was fruitless praying, we turned around and realized that the interim priest had been given by God to us, and was already fulfilling needs that lay outside our carefully crafted job description for the new priest, needs whose importance we had long overlooked.

When we or someone we love is suffering, when we are concerned about the real and immediate needs of the world around us, we hopefully get to a point where we can pray with clarity of intention, in faith and passion. Sometimes this is the tipping point, where God's desire matches our own, and new things come into being. But sometimes we are asking for things that cannot or will not take place, for reasons that will always remain hidden to us.

However, this does not mean that God has not responded. Instead of physical healing, we may be given freedom from fear and resentment. Instead of the poor not having to worry anymore about food and safety, a community of people is given a new passion for justice and a dignity that is not dependent upon prosperity. As St. Paul said, "All things work together for good for those who love God" (Romans 8:28). Even crucifixion, of which Jesus begged to be spared, worked toward the good of resurrection beyond the grave. God always answers prayer.

When we pray, our desire and God's desire mingle, so that a force begins to go to work. Deep within our souls, deep within a community of people, low stirrings are taking place that we cannot see. Something good always comes out of this hidden stirring of grace. "The kingdom of God is as if someone would scatter seed on the ground, and would sleep and rise night and day, and the seed would sprout and grow, he does not know how" (Mark 4:26–27). Who can explain how a seed becomes a tree? Who can explain how the crucifixion became the resurrection? Who can explain how tragedy and suffering in our lives become something good and powerful? The seed sprouts and grows, and we do not know how.

At one point, I prayed regularly for what I felt was a much-needed freedom of spirit, for joy and light in my life. It didn't come. Instead, I found myself confused, trapped even more vividly in very familiar patterns of anxiety, selfishness, and compulsive behavior. My problems increased. Much later I realized that God had answered my prayer, by making the very things that blocked my liberation more obvious, more intense. Only by this intensity could I then move through and beyond them.

It is not as if there is some divine Master Plan that denies this so that can happen, as if every detail fits into a puzzle: I didn't get my job of choice because God had this other, better one lined up for me already. This is the idea of predestination or fate, which leaves no room for chance or for human choice.

Rather, the whole universe is moving inexorably toward love and goodness and its fulfillment in God, and nothing will stop this motion. Bad things happen even when good people pray that they won't; but God is still at work, bringing good out of evil, stirring beneath the surface, responding to every situation with a new twist, a new turn toward love. God always answers prayer.

love everybody

The world works fairly well under a system of reward and punishment. For the most part, if we work hard, if we are honest, if we attend to our emotional and physical health and are fair and kind to other people, then good things will come our way. We'll have friends, enough money to live on, and things will generally go well for us. On the other hand, if we are lazy, dishonest, mean, and abusive to ourselves and others, things will not go so well. In religious, philosophical, and legal systems, this system of goodness/reward and evil/punishment is codified through ethics, law and morals.

But life is really not so simple, as we know. Sometimes nice guys finish last, and the wicked prosper. Fitness devotees die of cancer, good people suffer, and some get away with murder. When these things happen, we naturally do everything in our power to turn the tide back toward the proper moral order: we bring criminals to justice, we stand up for our rights, we seek out medical solutions for our illnesses, and we protect the innocent.

However, this doesn't always work. Sometimes we can't stop a cancer or prevent oppression. Innocent people are sent to death row. We can't ultimately control the system of reward and punishment for moral behavior.

It is at this point that religions and philosophies find a way of helping us deal with the pain of injustice. Ancient Jewish psalms cry for God to intervene, or point hopefully to an eventual outcome for the righteous and the wicked that will reestablish the moral order. Hindus and Buddhists believe in karma, where one builds up good or bad energy through one's actions, resulting in benefit or ruin for oneself in the future.

Jesus introduces into this mix something quite revolutionary: he tells us to love everybody. No matter what that person has done, no matter whether they deserve it or not, just love them. Give them what they *don't* deserve, reward them when they're *not* good, be kind to those who hate you, bless those who persecute you, forgive those who sin greatly, and be generous for no reason.

In dozens of parables and teachings, Jesus advised his followers to step out of the whole system of reward and punishment entirely, and just love without any justification for it whatsoever. He crossed the boundary of common sense and ethical systems, and moved his audience into a new world entirely, where the rules they normally lived by simply vanished.

It's almost as if, like a magician, Jesus stepped up and unhooked two parts of a chain that everyone assumes to be inseparable. He disengaged the one middle link that connects action to consequence, and lo and behold, divine love kept the second half of the chain suspended in the air, all on its own! The people were left in open-mouthed wonder, their minds racing to find a way to understand; all they could say was, "But . . . but . . . but. . . ."

In one story, workers who came at the eleventh hour to the job were paid the same as those who came early in the morning. In another, a returning ne'er-do-well son wasn't even given time to perform his well-rehearsed speech of shame and repentance before his father embraced him and called for a feast of love and thanksgiving. Jesus treated a notorious sinner like an honored guest at a banquet after she washed his feet with her tears. *Everyone* got the prize of forgiveness and love: oppressive Roman officials, small-minded religious legalists, women caught in adultery, tax-collecting collaborators with Rome, apostles who betrayed him, even the soldiers who crucified him. Those who witnessed this outrageous love could only respond, "But . . . but . . . but. . . ."

Jesus' unconditional love did not wipe away the necessity for justice and accountability. I'm sure that Jesus did not advocate, in the name of love, turning a blind eye to criminal activity or behavior that was destructive to others. Unconditional love was rather a kind of new dimension thrown into the mix, a radically different possibility that would sometimes completely alter the equation, break the logjam, and heal the participants.

The world saw a rare example of how both justice and undeserving love can exist side-by-side in the Truth and Reconciliation Commission in South Africa after the fall of apartheid. Accountability and truth were not casualties of love; they were handmaidens to it. Just like Jesus, who always named the sin before he unconditionally forgave it, those who had done great evil in South Africa were required to name to their victims and other witnesses exactly what they had done. They were required to face and hear how their actions affected others. Then they were released, scot-free. They had to come to the truth, but once they did, they were not held within the normal system of wrongdoing and punishment. They were held to the higher system of divine forgiveness.

Because the leaders of this movement were Christian—many of them Anglicans, including Archbishop Desmond Tutu—they knew that unconditional forgiveness, given in the context of accountability, would be the only thing that would heal their nation. If they insisted on the usual way of the world—revenge, punishment, imprisonment for crimes committed—the bitterness of their suffering would only increase. Like the family members who finally witness the execution of the one who murdered their loved one, they would find that there is really no peace in retribution. There is only peace and healing where, in the context of accountability and truth, love is exchanged for hatred.

This business of unconditional love, given to the undeserving, is an "unjust" economy, an assault on "common sense." That's why it is so hard, and why even Christian followers of Jesus so seldom use it. When we are wronged, it is humanly "natural" (and sometimes advisable) to fight so that right can prevail. But there comes a point where we must drop the fight and turn the tables, so that a different energy might enter into the mix. For love creates a new chemistry, new possibilities, new relationships.

It's easy to love those who are lovable, to be kind to those who are kind to us. That's natural, and not much needs to be said about it. Jesus asked, "Do not even the tax collectors do the same?" (Matthew 5:46). But as followers of Jesus, we are to be different, as he was different. We are to love everybody. We are to stop doing what we all normally do, which is to dole out our little love in a way that seems proportionate to what we think others deserve. We are simply to love, without reason.

This doesn't mean that we won't continue to feel anger, or actively pursue the righting of wrongs, or that we will naively make ourselves vulnerable to dangerous people, or that we will happily choose to spend time in the company of those who offend or hurt us.

It means that we won't hold anything against them, and that we will seek to do them good. We will pray for them—and pray not for God to correct them, but to bless them. We will treat them as if we don't even know anything bad about them: with dignity, respect, and fairness. We won't gossip or complain about them. When we speak of them, we might try to objectively describe what they've done, but we won't ascribe motivations to their actions. We won't give ourselves the bitter, poisonous satisfaction of condemning or ridiculing them and justifying ourselves. We won't hold ourselves above them. We'll know that we're capable of just as much wrongdoing, given the right circumstances, and that they're probably also capable of great good. Ours is not to judge such things.

How is such a stance possible? We certainly can't achieve it by deciding it is a good idea to do so. Unconditional love that is poured out upon others for no reason is not really a human trait; it is divine. And so we must rely upon God to accomplish it in us.

First of all, this means prayer. When we find ourselves unable to love someone else, we pray for ourselves and for them, that the Spirit might enter into this situation before it gets any worse. Humbling ourselves, we seek to understand our own part in creating an atmosphere that is lacking in complete love and harmony. We also pray that we might become acutely aware of any baggage we are carrying in the relationship—any buttons that are being pushed. Only with this awareness will the waters, muddied by emotion, settle and become clear.

At this point, we move from the prayer of humility, blessing, and dependence upon God's guidance and insight, to action. We begin to try to right the wrong, to reestablish harmony between us. Because only after we've come to a point of clarity where we are no longer influenced by ego-driven impulses, is it the right time to speak, to act, to express the truth we humbly believe. Kindness and honesty characterize this conversation, as well as a willingness to hear what the other feels and believes.

Then if the other responds in kind, wonderful! *And if not, wonderful!* Because at this point, our work regarding accountability is done, and all that is left is love. This is where the real work of God begins, of course: where we drop our justifications and our insistence upon others being the way we want them to be, and just love them as they are, without improvement. God is the one who loves at this point, because we cannot love this way on our own.

To become a vehicle for God's unconditional and healing love, we are required to shift our attention away from the circumstance or the relationship—or even the person we are called to love—and toward love itself. Our focus is no longer upon what the other person did, their reasons for it, our understanding of the situation, whatever good qualities we try to perceive in them, or even the imagined effect of our love. Our focus is solely upon love, which is another word for God.

The Dalai Lama speaks of this often in terms of *developing the capacity* for kindness, for goodness and for love. When we look within our heart and develop our own inner capacity for kindness, then it just comes out of us; it is not dependent upon circumstances that support it. When we pray for a growth of love and goodness within us, it is like a light that then simply shines. Jesus called us to develop this divine capacity within:

> so that you may be children of your Father in heaven; for
> he makes his sun rise on the evil and on the good, and
> sends rain on the righteous and on the unrighteous.
> (Matthew 5:45)

Like the sun, like the rain, divine love can then just come out of us, toward everyone, for no reason at all. And it is this radical love that will heal the world, and ourselves in the process.

face into conflict

I suppose some people enjoy conflict. They certainly seem to create a great deal of it. They give themselves over to contention with lusty abandon. But do they really like it? I don't. As a very young child, I had good reason to fear the conflict in my family around alcohol and eventual divorce; it was destructive. So I learned early on how to anticipate things, how to make myself invisible, or how to make subtle adjustments in relationships to prevent discord from taking place. When conflict came anyway, I felt anxious, out of sorts. I became an expert at moving quickly to restore equanimity.

Eventually this strategy fell apart. Marriage, kids, work—"the full catastrophe," as Zorba the Greek memorably said—all of this undermined my careful scheme. I couldn't avoid conflict any longer. The effort to manipulate others to prevent friction, the attempt to keep things smooth—this became transparently worse than the option of entering into the conflict. I gradually and painfully learned to trust the process of moving with others directly into the storm in its early phase, staying with it, feeling its surges, waiting, listening, coming back together and talking again, until truth could emerge and change could occur. I still feel anxious all the way through, but at least I am more likely to give myself over to the tempest until it runs its course.

We live in conflict. Some people seem to have (or create) more of it than others; sometimes in our lives it is more intense than other times. But it is never far away, for we don't live in the garden of Eden. We are very diverse, and we are imperfect. Our differences of desire, temperament, and personal and group history all contribute to the friction of human life. Besides, without conflict, there would never be creativity, problem-solving, or progress. To be alive is to experience conflict.

What do we do with this fact of life? Many work very hard to keep the peace at all costs. Others jump into the fray, damaging themselves and others as they thrash about. Some try to control the world around them and everyone in it. A few learn how to accept the conflict of life with grace, not avoiding or fearing it, dealing with the challenges it presents in a patient and constructive way.

For those of us who are religious, conflict presents some particular challenges. We might view conflict in our life, when it comes, as a spiritual failure: If I were truly enlightened, my life would be peaceful all the time. I wouldn't feel anxious or angry, and this situation wouldn't have deteriorated the way it did. Or we may justify whatever conflict comes along as proof of our God-given righteousness, refusing to look at our own part in having created it.

But there is another approach to conflict that is suggested by our Christian faith: to accept it as natural, move into it with as much love and truth as we can, exercise humility and self-examination as we do so, and entrust the whole thing into God's hands, not being attached to the outcome.

Conflict is to be expected for Christians. After all, we worship a man on a cross. Jesus was frequently at odds with others around him. He was executed by those who were threatened by his words and actions. And Jesus told us to take up our cross and follow him. Where? Into our own Calvary, our own conflicts. While the cross is a physical martyrdom for some in this world even today, for most of us it is less dramatic, but still difficult and often unpleasant, at least at first.

So taking up our cross means that we accept it as a natural and normal part of the life of faith. As followers of Jesus, sometimes our values, actions, and perspective will put us at odds with those around us. Living simply, we question rampant consumerism. Seeking reconciliation, we bring together opposites and put each person's sense of truth on the table. Defending the poor and working toward peace, we encounter those who defend privilege and power instead. Demanding spiritual authenticity, we come up against those who compromise or twist religion into something it was never meant to be. Including the outcast, we encounter the wrath of those who would rather judge them. Trying to remain faithful to what we feel called to do by a God to whom we owe ultimate allegiance, sometimes we become divided from those to whom we owe a lesser allegiance, even those we are close to.

Conflict is to be expected for the follower of Jesus. As he said,

> I came to bring fire to the earth, and how I wish it were already kindled! I have a baptism with which to be baptized, and what stress I am under until it is completed! Do you think that I have come to bring peace to the earth? No, I tell you, but rather division! From now on five in one household will be divided, three against two and two against three; they will be divided:
>> father against son
>>> and son against father,
>> mother against daughter
>>> and daughter against mother,
>> mother-in-law against her daughter-in-law
>>> and daughter-in-law against mother-in-law. (Luke 12:49–53)

Of course, we must be careful about this. Not every conflict is a result of our simplicity, our selfless efforts to create justice and truth, or our allegiance to a higher power. We don't always bring love, truth, and humility into conflict with us. Sometimes—in fact almost always—there is at least an element of our own imperfection in the works. We must avoid self-righteousness, always willing to admit and amend the ways in which we have contributed to conflict.

And yet even if we do engage in conflict with love and humility, we will still at times be set against others. The question then becomes: Can we trust the tension as potentially creative and life-giving, rather than a threat? A positive answer to this question really depends upon faith. For if we entrust ourselves to God in the midst of difficulty, if we have faith, then we will know that the Spirit is at work in and among us, always working to create life. With faith, conflict becomes not a sign of failure or something that has to be quickly "fixed"; it is part of the natural tension of life which the Spirit enters and transforms.

For the follower of Jesus, taking up our cross involves surrender to a power that is greater than our own will, a power that is always at work within and among us. On his own cross, Jesus abandoned himself into God's trust: "Father, into your hands I commend my spirit" (Luke 23:46). As he surrendered himself into God's care, the Spirit was at work to bring life out of this most horrendous of conflicts, to bring life even out of miserable failure and death.

For us, to surrender does not mean to passively give up. It means that we entrust ourselves to the One who is Life. We walk into the storm of conflict, as Jesus did, not so much with bravery as with trust. It is this kind of surrendered confidence that Jesus tried to communicate to his followers before he left them, knowing the difficulty which they would be facing as his followers:

> The hour is coming, indeed it has come, when you will be scattered, each one to his home, and you will leave me alone. Yet I am not alone because the Father is with me.

I have said this to you, so that in me you may have peace. In the world you face persecution. But take courage; I have conquered the world! (John 16:32–33)

Surrender also means that we are not attached to the outcome of the conflict in which we are engaged. We don't have to win, because God ultimately wins it all. God has conquered the world. If we do our best to bring love and truth and self-reflection into the difficulties we face, good *will* come out of it. It is not ours to predetermine what that good will look like. We put in our effort to be honest and strong, we try to remain humble and loving, we surrender it all to God, and let the chips fall where they may.

death is not the enemy

all over the Roman Empire, criminals and supposed enemies of the state were brutally beaten, hung on a cross to slowly die in agony, and then left to be ravaged by animals and the elements. The message was clear: don't even think about doing what this person did, or the same will happen to you. It was a gruesome public spectacle of humiliation and domination.

And yet this cruel method of torturous execution became for Christians a sign of hope, glory, and peace. What a paradox! For all over the world, millions look at the cross and see not defeat, violence, and degradation, but forgiveness, love and victory. As St. Paul said, "It is sown in dishonor, it is raised in glory" (1 Corinthians 15:43).

How did the early Christians end up centering everything around this amazing paradox? How did they experience it in their lives, so convinced of its power that it changed them forever, gave them hope and courage in times of persecution, and launched this unstoppable gospel into every corner of the world for centuries to come? How do we take hold of this amazing and powerful paradox? Where do we let it work in our lives, and what is it really like to move from defeat and loss into hope and victory?

Imagine the setting on the first Holy Week. As Jesus' mission began to unravel and his enemies coalesced into action, things started to look really bleak. The disciples no doubt felt the clammy fog of disaster closing in around them. When Jesus was arrested, beaten, crucified and finally dead, all hope was lost. The wonders of miraculous healings, the joy of bread multiplied, the rush of eager crowds, the freedom of social norms being shattered, the astonishing pearls of wisdom coming from Jesus' mouth—all of this now gone, trampled in the mud, lifeless. Ahead of them lay nothing but despair: continuing Roman brutality, poverty, and the rigidity of the religious elite.

And then, three days later, Jesus was back with them. However, the tremendous joy and relief they felt were to be very short-lived. Because after just a short few weeks, he was gone again! Now they had to live permanently with a very strange situation. For even though the risen Christ promised always to be with them spiritually, nothing would ever be the same. They were never again to enjoy the quiet sunny afternoons by the shores of Galilee, listening to their teacher, healing the sick, discovering the freedom that was so fresh and exciting back then. That was over, done.

And now they were thrust into the unknown emerging life of the church, on their own together, with only an intuitive grasp of Jesus' spiritual presence, which they hoped would sustain them on the journey ahead. They hadn't signed up for this kind of adventure, but there it was.

As the months and then years stretched forward, the early church came to know this new reality—Jesus' resurrected presence among them—and all that it meant. It wasn't a sudden understanding. It was like the presence of something invisible, undefined, amorphous, something slowly coming into being, shaping them as it did. It was only over a long period of time that life with the resurrected Jesus took the final shape we have come to recognize today. They had to struggle through decades—even centuries—of uncertainty, persecution, doubt, and theological argumentation among the ranks. Today, millions of people just assume that Jesus is spiritually present in our Eucharist, prayer life, community, and ministry. But for the early Christians it took years to really believe and experience this as reality.

What they finally understood was that the horrible crucifixion of Jesus, the end of their lives as they knew them, and in fact *any and all such traumas and difficulties*—these things are the crucible in which God's Spirit begins to create new life. Things go badly, something happens that changes our life forever, we suffer, but slowly something new, something resurrected begins to emerge.

Things happen in life: One day we go to work and are laid off; our spouse has an affair; or our child is diagnosed with breast cancer. We suffer. But as we abide with God through our dark times, something inside will stir to life. We discover enlivening parts of ourselves that we had allowed to be squelched in our previous vocation; we find a more honest relationship and new passion with our spouse; we stop taking our daughter for granted, rejoicing in each day that we have with her. Perhaps it will take us a long time (as it did for the early church) to perceive this new thing, to trust it and come to enjoy it, but it will come. In the process of becoming, we will be (again, like the early church) at odds and unable to understand. But in the end God will not disappoint us. New life will gradually come.

This is the paradoxical mystery of the Christian faith at its heart: Suffering and death are not the end; they are not the enemy. They are instead a crucible in which something new slowly comes into being. That's why the early Christians placed the mysterious paradox of the gruesome crucifixion and joyous resurrection at the center. They had discovered the secret of life! It was their mission, then, to hold up this paradoxical secret for all the world to see.

In the last few years I have been undergoing a kind of death and resurrection. With our children leaving home and becoming independent, something very precious and good is over, never to return in the same way. As much as we've enjoyed the quiet and freedom of being just the two of us as a couple again, we've been off balance too, trying to cope with both the loss and the new reality. We're still in a time of emerging transformation. We're aging; lots of things are shifting; we're making changes.

So I'm learning to trust that this is a time for the cross and the resurrection, that God is, in fact, very active in a hidden way, working to bring new life in ways that I am unable to perceive or even imagine. I cannot control the timing or the outcome of this transformation, so I must trust in the God of gradual resurrection.

You no doubt have similar personal experiences of your own. A divorce, an accident, a diagnosis, a tragic loss, a fall into depression, a turning point, a Good Friday that changed everything forever. In such times you are launched into unknown territory, and it is therefore helpful to bring back to mind the first disciples. Yes, they must have been overjoyed on the first Easter. But then it began to sink in. Jesus would now only be with them in Spirit. They were launched into a new and unknown territory.

In this setting they held up the cross and resurrection of Jesus as their banner, as their central paradoxical mystery that did not explain, but rather brought hope to their struggle to evolve. For as they held up this gruesome spectacle of execution as the sign of hope, they were saying: Even this, even the worst thing that life can hand us—this is the crucible where God goes to work. It may take time to understand our new life as Christians living together with Jesus in spirit, but resurrection will come.

Perhaps you are in just such a time now, a long in-between time. Really, all of life is made up of such times, and there is nothing permanent other than God. In one way or another, we're always ending, grieving, then hoping, struggling ahead into the mystery of the new. And so our spiritual work is to become comfortable with impermanence.

The cross helps us to trust in this fact of life, to trust that God is at work in this crucible of the unknown. Loss and change are not the enemy. They are only the beginning for a God who makes all things new. And they are only the beginning for people of faith who embrace this mystery.

be a prophet

The biblical prophets were not crystal-ball gazers. For the most part, they didn't concern themselves with the far-off future. When they spoke in metaphors of stars, beasts, and devils, they weren't foreseeing the modern world's fall of communism or atomic weapons or the pollution of the earth.

Instead, they looked around and read the signs of their own times. As Israel journeyed through history, the prophets, like wary scouts, sniffed the air, detected a whiff (or a stench) of things gone wrong, and warned their people of what might come if they kept on going in the direction that they were headed. Prophets such as Jeremiah usually alerted people, especially the ruling elite, not of their personal moral failings but of the consequences that would come upon all the people because of the leaders' sins of injustice and corruption. This kind of prophet was often dark and angry about the world he found himself inhabiting.

John the Baptist is considered by Christians to be the last in this line of dark prophets. He railed against Pharisees and Sadducees, religious leaders, who came to him for baptism: "You brood of vipers! Who warned you to flee from the wrath to come? Bear fruit worthy of repentance" (Matthew 3:7b–8). By calling upright religious authorities a nest of snakes, he didn't exactly endear himself to the powers that be. In fact, he eventually lost his head when the Herod family had had enough of his ranting.

This angry prophet, who stood in the line of all the others before him, was the one to usher in the coming of the Messiah: his cousin, Jesus of Nazareth. Jesus was probably one of his followers until John baptized him, when Jesus moved forward into his own identity, ministry, and leadership. So the dark prophets were an important element of Jesus' coming into being.

When Jesus spoke against the powerful who oppressed the widow and orphan, he became darkly prophetic. When he entered Jerusalem, he wept over the blindness of the people who refused to listen to the prophets who came before him, even as he knew that he too would soon die a prophet's death. When Jesus overturned the money changers' tables in the Temple, he was making a prophetic, political statement about power and social control through religion.

But the Hebrew prophets were also light. They sensed the overarching love of God for humankind in history, knowing that everything was ultimately held in the Creator's hands, that no matter what calamities might befall us, all would eventually be well. Even though they might not know the specific time or nature of this outcome, prophets such as Isaiah used mythological language to paint a picture of God's ultimate victory over injustice, sin, evil, and death. Certain prophets were light, hopeful.

Jesus' coming as Messiah was ushered in by these prophets of light, too. For while the original prophetic authors may have believed that their songs of hope referred to figures in their own age or the near future, Christians have always interpreted their dreams as prefiguring Jesus: "For a child has been born for us, a son given to us . . . and he is named Wonderful Counselor, Mighty God, Everlasting Father, Prince of Peace" (Isaiah 9:6). So the prophets of light had something to do with Jesus, too, at least in the eyes of the Christian community.

When the story of Jesus' birth was told, it was said that everything happened according to the prophets of hope and light: in the line of David, born of a virgin, in Bethlehem, to

Nazareth. When he stood on the Mount of Transfiguration (Matthew 17), he was accompanied by Moses for the Law and Elijah for the Prophets, as a heavenly voice said, "This is my Son . . . listen to him" (v.5)—listen to this one who is bathed in light as the fulfillment of the prophets of hope. When Jesus confidently healed the sick as a sign of God's coming kingdom, he pointed to the long-awaited day when there will be no more sickness, sin, injustice, or death.

We normally associate religion, especially "spirituality," with the light side, with kind and gentle voices and actions, with peace and kindness, tolerance and humility. We claim that hatred shall be overcome only by love, and rightly so. But when these values of hope are not balanced by the dark side of the prophets' message, something gets out of balance. For sometimes people and movements must be stopped; injustice, greed and oppression must be named for what they are. And rather than polarize these tendencies, separating the hopeful prophets of light from the angry dark ones, the prophetic voice is at its best when it finds some kind of equilibrium between the two.

St. Francis is remembered for his love of animals, but he was also the one who preached against materialism and cared for the outcasts of society. Malcolm X is known for his fiery speeches that incited some to violence, but his anger was also a wake-up call for a reluctant, racist nation; Eleanor Roosevelt was an outspoken, strong-willed woman; she was also a compassionate champion of the downtrodden. Gandhi is recalled as a kindly little man in a loincloth who urged non-violence, but he was also the first to cry out unrelentingly against British oppression.

The best of all our prophets point the finger *and* lift up our hearts in hope. They name what is evil and they lead us toward the good. They read the signs of the times, warning us to forsake our wicked ways, and they trust in the eventual victory of light and harmony. Each prophet finds him- or herself somewhere on the continuum between darkness and light, some leaning more toward one than the other. But the healthy and helpful ones always contain something of both, as Jesus did.

Who are the prophets of our day? Who are the scouts, sniffing the air, detecting and naming the stench of something gone wrong? Who is pointing us toward a better, more hopeful way? Are you willing to heed them? Perhaps more important, are you willing to *be* prophetic, to read the signs of the times with both a skeptic's wisdom and a believer's hope? Do you follow Jesus' example—as he asked of his disciples—to be "wise as serpents and innocent as a doves" (Matthew 10:16)?

It's difficult to hold in tension these two polarities of prophetic warning and hope. It's easier to let the balance go and fall toward one or the other: cynicism or naiveté. In debates with our friends, we either defend a hopeful position or we play the devil's advocate. The nuanced view is hard to maintain. But it is more faithful to the way life is; it is more faithful to the example of the Hebrew prophets, including Jesus. It is easy to be a flag-waver in America; it is easy to mutter darkly against the political/corporate interests. It is harder, but more faithful, to affirm both America's goodness and its blind spots.

So when you see injustice, name it, try to stop it. When greed, addiction and idolatry threaten to overtake your nation or your home, tell others where you believe this path will lead. When self-righteous, arrogant and selfish impulses run over others who are less aggressive, speak for the one who has no voice. Don't be afraid to enter the darkness and name it for what it is. Be engaged in the world, facing into its problems and suffering.

But balance your outrage with transcendent hope and light. Remember that nothing will separate us from the love of God or the ultimate victory of good. Rest in this faith, so that your anger doesn't become clinging, desperately having to change things in order to avert that which you fear. Drop your impulse to control the effects of your words and actions, knowing that the eventual outcome is in the hands of the One who is love. Be a prophet of both darkness and light.

heal and be healed

Perhaps for more than anything else, Jesus was known in his lifetime as a healer. People also knew that he taught, that he challenged people's assumptions, that he spoke to power with an inner authority. But the crowds came out because he healed people. In fifty-five passages from the gospels, we are told that he was followed, pressed upon, even hounded by great crowds of people seeking healing.

> Jesus went throughout Galilee, teaching in their synagogues and proclaiming the good news of the kingdom and curing every disease and every sickness among the people. So his fame spread throughout all Syria, and they brought to him all the sick, those who were afflicted with various diseases and pains, demoniacs, epileptics, and paralytics, and he cured them. And great crowds followed him from Galilee, the Decapolis, Jerusalem, Judea, and from beyond the Jordan. (Matthew 4:23–25)

This was the story of those three years of public ministry. Everywhere he went, people had heard of his healing powers. They came in hope, expecting a miracle. It seems, however, that very few today receive the kind of miraculous healing that Jesus performed in Galilee. And yet it does happen. After much prayer, cancer miraculously disappears, and doctors cannot explain it. I witnessed, during a powerful healing liturgy, a woman afflicted with macular degeneration who was able to see very clearly for several hours; it was a kind of temporary gift from God, perhaps intended to inspire faith.

It seems that even fewer people are given the gift of being able to heal others. The possibility of this gift is a powerful temptation, and many fall prey to it. Televangelists call out body parts they imagine in their minds, and people from the audience claim to be the one whose afflictions are seen and then healed. People line up to be touched by the preacher, falling backwards or bursting into holy laughter at the predictable moment. All of this makes us cynical about those who claim to be healers.

And yet there are those who have been used by God to heal others. One time (among a small handful of such times in my twenty-four years of ordained ministry) I was used in such a way. A woman had a terrible condition of internal pain and bleeding that was sapping the life out of her. She had been to doctors and nothing seemed to be working. She was losing weight, strength, and hope. She came to a regular Sunday Eucharist at my church, and when I approached her in order to share the Peace—as I was doing, as normal, with lots of others—she said she saw me wrapped in a golden light, and my touch warmed her right through. I felt nothing at the time. I didn't even know her. She was immediately and completely healed of her physical illness. The doctors could not explain it.

I know that I cannot conjure up such moments. I suppose I could have gone on the road with a healing schtick, but I have preferred to let such moments happen by God's hand. Perhaps others have been healed in such a sacramental moment of the community, without my knowledge. Miraculous healing does take place.

But usually, it is not so dramatic. Medication and medical care are sought, delivered, and usually they work to make the person better. Sometimes illnesses go on, taking the lives of perfectly faithful and prayerful people. Why? Is God capricious, stingy with grace? Or are the supposed miraculous healings of a few a mere delusion, or some weird aberration of the physics of matter, the evidence of chaos theory?

I don't pretend to know the answer to these questions. But I do know that sometimes people are healed miraculously. Healing does not seem to be related to the urgency of their prayer or the depth of their faith. It just happens. Or more often, it doesn't.

Or does it?

That depends on what we assume "healing" means. Are we looking for just one acceptable result from our prayers, or are we open to all kinds of possibilities? Perhaps a request for physical healing from illness might result in the healing of a relationship instead, before death makes such a healing impossible. Perhaps through daily prayers for healing, we eventually learn to transcend our fears and we move into a freer mode of existence.

Whatever the results, we are not in control of them. Our work as people of faith is to present ourselves to God as we are and ask for his love. Period. Anything beyond this is an attempt to control, to manipulate, to understand things we cannot understand, to take over the work that belongs to God. Like the crowds that pressed upon Jesus, our work is to show up, present our needs before God, and ask for his love. Period.

Healing will come. On this we can count. *Something* good will come of our faith and our prayer. God will not ignore us. Since it is only in hindsight that we can see the action of grace in our lives, we should not waste one minute imagining or questioning what might happen to us in the future as a result of our prayer in the present. Just show up, pray, and wait with an open mind.

As followers of Jesus, we are also to be healers of others. Like the disciples, we are sent out to heal in Jesus' name. Like my experience in liturgy with the woman at the sharing of the Peace, we are called to be instruments of God's grace, and often without knowing we are being used in this way. In fact, chances are that the more we think we know that God is using us, the more our ego is in play and the less active God is able to be.

So how do we heal others, if not by deciding to do so? By living a life grounded in God. If we remain grounded in God, our hearts will be made truer, our intentions clearer. We will love more selflessly, and we will care about others more deeply. Grounded in God, we will become a walking presence of God here on earth. When we touch, when we love, when we pray for others, when we give of ourselves to the world around us we will be communicating the very energy of the Spirit. God will flow out from our heart, into the world around us. As we become ever more grounded in God, less ego and less fear will stand in the way of God's freedom of operation. Such is the way that God works to heal through us.

Our healing of others is not limited to personal relationships of prayer, love, and touch. When we are grounded in God, we are also a presence of divine healing in the wider world, affecting people we don't even know. Our grounding keeps the energy of divine grace flowing around us, beyond us, touching people in the world in ways we can never be aware of. If we are all connected through the physics of matter, if we are all connected in the one Spirit, then how we live certainly affects the world around us. Our life of prayer and faith is not a private matter. It affects everyone, everything.

God-through-us affects the strangers we brush against, in how we smile or how we carry ourselves. God-through-us affects national domestic and foreign policy by how we vote, by how we attempt to influence our elected representatives. God-through-us affects the planet as we attempt to live in harmony with it.

Jesus lived as a healer in order to communicate dramatically, by his very life, that God heals. God heals you and me, and God heals others through us. God is the very energy of life, of love, of renewal and goodness. And the more we give ourselves to this energy, the more we are healed and are used to heal others.

who do you say
that he is?

after Jesus and his disciples had been moving through Galilee publicly, healing and teaching, he took his friends aside and asked them what people were saying about him. What had they overheard? "Who do they say that I am?" (Mark 8:27; see Matthew 16:15, Luke 9:18) The disciples said, well, some say John the Baptist, some say Elijah or one of the prophets come back again. Jesus then penetrated them with a look and asked, "But who do you say that I am?" (Mark 8:29)

Jesus asks the same of everyone who would be a follower of his. He asks all who call themselves Christian, after his own title, *the Christ, the Anointed One*. Who do *you* say that Jesus is? For some, the answer is easy; it is a theological position: Jesus died for my sins and I believe in him. This is basically an intellectual answer, a reply that is dogmatic in nature. But what does that mean, really? What difference does Jesus make, if any, in that person's daily life?

Others of us settle for a very personalized, sometimes sentimental answer, as in the familiar hymn: "He walks with me, and he talks with me, and he tells me I am his own."

Some Christians whose connection with the faith is merely cultural keep him at a distance, as a kindly but very vague presence. Jesus is just there in the background, unmoving, like a mountain range off in the distance. Why would you question the reality of the mountains? They are just a fact of life, a part of the spiritual landscape. But again, what difference does that background presence make, if any, in that person's daily life?

But what about us? What about you?

There are many ways in which we can enter into a relationship with Jesus, but two are of particular interest to me. Both of them have been taught throughout the church's history, right from the start. One really emphasizes Christ's divinity, the other his humanity. One is mystical, one is practical. Neither one is better than the other, just different. At times, one approach may make more sense to us than the other, and so that is the one, for a time, that we should pursue. For most of us, the pursuit of both paths is not sequential at all; we apply elements of both simultaneously.

St. Paul told us that all those who are baptized are clothed in Christ, that we belong to him. As it says in the baptismal rite, you are now marked as Christ's own forever. We are anointed with oil in baptism, *chrismated*, made Christly, Christian, like the original Anointed One, the Christ. We are of Christ.

Paul went so far as to say that it was no longer he who lived, but Christ in him. He had died to his old self; now Christ was living through him. This is the mystical, divine, spiritual presence of the Son of God who dwells within. In fact, this is the approach that Paul takes to Christ throughout his letters. He is really not concerned at all with the human Jesus, how he was born, or even what he taught. Christ is for Paul the life-changing interior spiritual presence of God. This is the approach I emphasized in my last book, which is titled *Becoming Christ*.

And how do we become Christ, or perhaps more accurately, how do we let him become us? There are many ways. It is the faith of the church that when we are baptized, we really do take Christ on; we really do belong to him from that point forward. We can invite him into our hearts; we can pray to him. We can sit or kneel in any sacramental church and pray before the reserved sacrament, where we believe that the Christ is truly present in the consecrated bread and wine. We can take his presence into our very bodies, as we consume his body and blood in the Eucharist. We can say the Jesus prayer, repeating his holy name as a mantra, slowly building a sense of his presence within. We can gaze into his face as we pray before an icon.

When we seek this kind of a relationship with Jesus, what happens? He really does begin to live through us. We become what we are made in baptism: Christly. As this happens over time, gradually his priorities, or what we call his will, become our will. When we develop a dynamic, daily relationship with the indwelling, divine Christ, we gradually find ourselves more like him. He slowly removes our obstacles to his freedom of movement within us. We then find ourselves surprisingly more able to forgive, to love unconditionally, to question our idols and attachments, to care deeply for those who suffer, and live into that awakened state he called the kingdom of God.

Then there is the more human, practical approach to a relationship with Jesus the man, the teacher. This was the kind of relationship his disciples had with him, which is still possible for us. It has to do with following Jesus where he leads us. He is the perfect human, who leads those who follow him into a more perfected humanity. This approach is the subject of the present book.

In this kind of a relationship with the human Jesus, we ponder his teachings in the gospels. We listen to his questions, demands, or actions as if they are happening to us. Feed the poor. Love your enemy. Repent. Trust in God. Give your money away. Pray for what you need. Gather the outcast. Hearing these teachings as if they are addressed directly to us, we take them in deeply, and do our best to respond to them.

We were given by God a wonderful and powerful gift in our creation: free will. As humans, we can choose how we shall live. We can choose to head down one of various roads that lead to self-centered isolation or generous interdependence, resentment or kindness, legalism, or freedom of spirit. In order to make these choices every day, we look for some sort of standard, some guidelines.

As Christians, Jesus' teachings must be our highest standard: not personal preferences, or patriotism, or the bottom line on a balance sheet, or political ideology, or a psychological model, or scientific logic, or conventional wisdom, or any other idol. Jesus is our chief guide, and we are called to follow.

As Albert Schweitzer put it so eloquently at the turn of the last century, in his book *The Quest of the Historical Jesus*:

> He comes to us as one unknown, without a name, as of old, by the lakeside, he came to those men who did not know who he was. He says the same words: "Follow me!" and sets us to those tasks which he must fulfil in our time. He comes. And to those who hearken to him, whether wise or unwise, he will reveal himself in the peace, the labours, the conflicts and the suffering that they may experience in his fellowship, and as an ineffable mystery they will learn who he is. (Minneapolis: Fortress Press, 2001, p. 487)

And yet, following Jesus is not simply a matter of following his rules, as if we could accomplish Christliness by being obedient to a moral guidebook. Rather, becoming a follower of Jesus means that we enter a path of inner transformation. Jesus did not simply demand that people do the right thing. Instead, he challenged people to be changed, from the inside out.

For when we follow Jesus, we will not only learn who he is, as Schweitzer put it. We will also be changed. Over time, we will be conformed to his character through his grace. In relationship with him, he works on us, and our will begins to be aligned with Jesus' will. For we are always shaped by whatever it is to which we give ourselves in this life. If we care most about money, its demands and values will drive us. If we care most about security or national interests or a brilliant mind, the values of those disciplines will shape us until we are made into their image. It is the same with Jesus. If we apply our will to Jesus' teachings, if we follow him, he will affect us, and we will gradually become like him.

So the result is the same, whether we become Christ by seeking him internally or whether we follow his teachings and become more fully human. In either case, we become more like him, which is the whole point of the Christian journey.

This is no sunny walk in the park. At times it might be that, but this journey will also require a darker, more demanding struggle. Right after Peter answered Jesus' question "Who do you say that I am?" by saying, "The Messiah of God," Jesus immediately spoke of suffering, rejection, death, and resurrection (Luke 9:20). He didn't only speak of these things for himself. He said, "If any want to become my followers, let them also deny themselves and take up their cross daily and follow me. For those who want to save their life will lose it, and those who lose their life for my sake will save it" (Luke 9:23–24).

The pivotal point of a relationship with Jesus Christ is this: spiritual death and resurrection. As St. Paul said, "I have been crucified with Christ; and it is no longer I who live, but it is Christ who lives in me" (Galatians 2:19–20). Whether we relate to Jesus as the divine, spiritual presence within, or whether we try to follow him with our will and our actions, our relationship with him will lead us to the cross and the resurrection, and that pivotal encounter will change us.

This paschal mystery will happen not just once, but many times in different ways. We will have to die as we put aside our own preferences and little personal dramas in the service of the greater good, as we deal with our addictions and attachments, as we suffer, as we are confronted with all our stubborn sins. It is always very difficult to deny ourselves, to die to self, which is why so many don't dare enter into a real relationship with Jesus.

But the Christ within will also make us new people. We will resurrect with Jesus as he makes possible what we cannot do: to love everyone without reason, to trust deeply, to be awake, free, and generously alive. This is the joy that those who keep him at arm's length will never know.

Jesus asks you, "Who do you say that I am?" You can satisfy yourself with a superficial answer: a theological idea, a sentimental picture, or a bland acknowledgment of his background presence. Or you may have answered the question in a more authentic way long ago, but now you have evolved, and the old answer no longer really helps you. Or you might just shrug the question off, thinking that you never have known what a relationship with Jesus might be like, and never will know.

But remember this: You belong to him. If you are a Christian, you were baptized into him. You were anointed as he was, made Christly, Christian. You are clothed with him. So reenter your relationship with Jesus that began at your baptism. Reawaken his presence, by praying to him or reading again his teachings in the gospels. Listen to his voice. Let him make himself known to you. Go with him through your own crosses and resurrections, as difficult as they may be. Become more like him, that together we might all enter with Jesus into the kingdom of God.

help the poor

drive or walk through any city and see homeless men and women begging on the streets. Turn on the television and hear about the poorest, most marginal people in the world who are ground down even further by circumstances of war, ethnic hatred, famine, or flood. Visit a nursing home and look into the eyes of an elderly, frail, lonely woman lost in the ravages of Alzheimer's disease. Go to a church food pantry and see the families waiting, waiting, as they are used to doing so often, for something to help them get by for another few days. Remember the children who are shuttled around from foster parent to social worker to new school and strange kids who will never be friends. Think of the millions of mothers and girlfriends who know that in a few years most of the angry young men they now know will be either locked away in a prison or dead.

It's all so overwhelming. Sometimes we would rather not even think about it. A realtor friend of mine tells me that some of his clients who move into our city ask him to find not only a gated community, but one that is located somewhere that will enable them to come and go from work and the gym in a way that they won't ever have to be exposed to unpleasant neighborhoods. We may not go this far, but we certainly try to avoid a nightly exposure to murder and tragedy on the ten o'clock news right before we go to sleep. It's just too much.

We may think of this as a modern phenomenon, and

certainly the media coverage of it is, but there is nothing new about proximity to lots of suffering people. In ages past, most people saw a great deal of poverty, illness, cruelty, and death. It was a reality of their daily lives, as it is of ours. So how are we supposed to deal with it?

A few pour themselves into some kind of work with those who suffer. Driven to *do* something about what they see, at an early age they find themselves drawn into tireless efforts on the behalf of the most vulnerable. Others turn their heads away, justifying their own self-centered existence by a kind of Calvinistic materialism: The poor are just lazy and immoral, and their poverty is the consequence of their own lack of character.

Many others of us try to give what we can to charity. We feel something and pray for those who are suffering. We contribute some time to individuals or projects that will help those around us who are in need. But we are still disturbed, because we know that the little bit we do will never be enough, that it is charity and not justice. On the other hand, when we hear Jesus' call to the rich young man to sell all his possessions and give the money to the poor, we know that this isn't a general commandment meant to be taken literally by everyone. We wish we could get to a more comfortable place with the fact of the world's suffering.

But suffering is something about which we are not meant to be comfortable. We can't make it all better, and we also can't just callously ignore it. So we have to live in this tension of feeling the pain of others' situations and knowing that our efforts will never be enough, and yet having to do *something*. How did Jesus deal with this tension?

We all know that Jesus cared deeply and constantly for the most vulnerable, and that he demanded that his followers do the same. He reached out to and healed the sick, comforted the mourning, had compassion on the crowds who were like sheep without a shepherd, forgave the shameful sinner, loved the unlovable, and brought the lowest person out of their isolation into the center, to the head of the table.

Jesus then turned to his disciples and said, "Go and do

likewise" (Luke 10:37). He linked worship of God with practical acts of charity, saying that if we didn't feed the hungry, visit the sick, and clothe the naked, we were refusing to serve him, since he dwells in these people (Matthew 25:31–46). He said that the most vulnerable among us, the children, must not be pushed away and never abused—for it would be better to have a huge stone tied around our neck and be thrown into the sea than to do that (Mark 9:42). He sent his disciples out to do as he did, to heal the sick and release the burdened through forgiveness. And yes, he told us to sell our empty possessions and give alms, so that we would have lasting spiritual treasure that—unlike worldly treasure—would always enrich us and never wear out (Luke 12:33). Most of all, he urged us to have compassion, to open our hearts and feel for those who are hurting and lost, and then be moved to do something for them.

Yet for all this practical compassion, he also knew that even he and his disciples could not make it all better. He didn't heal everyone in every village. After he left, people still got sick and suffered hunger After a period of intense work, he withdrew to a quiet place, away from the needy crowds, to be refreshed and renewed, and then moved on to the next town. He attended weddings and feasts and parties, no doubt paid for by people with some means. And he reminded his disciples that "you will always have the poor with you" (Mark 14:7), so that they could have a little perspective about their good works.

So Jesus didn't ask everyone to sell everything they owned—just one rich young man who was very attached to his wealth (Matthew 19:16–22). We can assume that he expected of the rest of us a more practical level of charitable giving. He didn't become so consumed with the needs of those who suffer that he neglected to take care of himself. He never lost his capacity to enjoy the good things of life. And he recalled us to the fact that there will always be those who are poor and suffering, in order that we might learn how to do what we can and let go of the rest, entrusting them to the care of God and other good-hearted people.

There are those who are compelled to become like Mother Teresa of Calcutta or Francis of Assisi or Dorothy Day, gladly renouncing all comfort and living selflessly among the poor, pouring their lives out for the most vulnerable in our society. But most of us are called to a more moderate lifestyle, with a home and a family to care for and enjoy. Most of us are called to do what we can for the poor and others who are hurting, and then to also take care of ourselves, savor the good things that life can give us, and let go of our inability to eliminate all suffering around us.

Yet as Mother Teresa herself used to suggest to those who put her on a pedestal, "Surely there is someone in your family, your neighborhood, or your church who is lonely, sick, or somehow in need of your love." We may not be able to save the world, but surely we can pay attention to the children and the elderly with whom we come in contact. We can feel some of the pain that we see on the nightly news, and we can pray for those people whose stories fill our heart with sorrow. We can refuse to turn away from this pain, and stop trying to find a comfortable resolution to something about which we are not meant to be comfortable. We can regularly give away a percentage of the income and comparative wealth we enjoy. We can support taxes that will provide a safety net for the most vulnerable among us, and economic policies that will build up the poor.

Never free from this responsibility to give generously to those who are less fortunate than ourselves, we *are* our brothers' and sisters' keepers. Christ is always standing before us there in the disguise of those who suffer, waiting for us to decide whether we shall respond to him or ignore him.

But beyond that, we can let go. We can unburden ourselves from the weight of the world, because it is not ours to carry. It is God's beautiful, broken world, and God will continue to care for it, using the hearts and hands of many others long after we are gone.

how to pray

J esus didn't say much about how we should pray. True, he did respond to his disciples' request, "Lord, teach us to pray," (Luke 11:1) by giving them a prayer, the "Lord's Prayer." Many books have been written on this prayer, a chapter for every phrase, each one teasing out the depths of this succinct teaching. "Our Father (community, intimacy) in heaven (eternal, transcendent), hallowed be your Name (praise, adoration). . . ." The prayer moves from praise to a plea for God's kingdom to come, to a request for daily needs and for forgiveness, and so on.

But what else did Jesus teach about how we should pray? He was a man of few words on the subject. He seemed to be far more concerned about how we live our faith than exactly how we should pray. And yet he did not neglect prayer; his life was suffused with it. While he may have not taught a great deal about techniques of prayer, he shared a great deal, both in word and in action, about the quality, the character of prayer.

Jesus' prayer was the kind of prayer that will disappoint those who are systematic in their approach to spirituality. The gospels do not report that Jesus had a Rule of Life that each day included intercession, petition, adoration, oblation, and confession, an hour of contemplation, and a recitation of the Daily Offices. There's nothing wrong with the development of a systematic spirituality, in fact some people are well-suited for it, but apparently Jesus was not one of them.

By contrast, the prayer of Jesus was simple, unsophisticated, a natural part of everyday life. Like a child, we are to be spontaneous in our prayer; for Jesus' prayer was spontaneously interwoven with his everyday life. His style, his "discipline of prayer" was to naturally drop into prayer as the circumstances of his life demanded. When someone needed healing, he prayed for healing. When someone needed to be forgiven, he forgave them. When the crowds needed feeding, he blessed God and the food and fed them. When he was tempted or when he suffered, he turned to God in prayer and simple trust. When he needed some solitude, he withdrew into quiet prayer.

The goal of any spirituality, any discipline of prayer, is to get to the point where we do this. The goal is to become so intimate with God that whatever life brings our way, we open our heart in prayer. When we suffer, we pray for help; when we feel grateful, we give thanks; when we are sick, we pray for healing; when we fall, we confess; when we consider the beauty of nature, we adore the Creator; when we carry the burden of concern for someone we love, we intercede.

Life has a way of presenting us with opportunities for prayer every moment. A "life of prayer" is therefore simply a transparency to the divine in everyday life. This is the purpose of all practices and disciplines of prayer: to be spontaneously responsive to God in life.

And yet, Jesus also took intentional time for prayer. As a person of prayer, he not only spontaneously responded to life's circumstances with supplication and praise; he also went off by himself for special minutes and hours of deliberate prayer. In many instances in the gospels, Jesus walked away from his friends, to a quiet place, a deserted place, to a mountain, always outdoors, where he could spend time in solitude with God. We don't know how he prayed at these times, but we do know that as busy as he was, as demanding and critical as the human needs around him were, he took time to be with God.

Sometimes we busy people say to ourselves that we don't need intentional times of prayer, that this is a kind of artificial construct anyway, that we dwell in the presence of God constantly as we go through our day. True enough, perhaps. But we then find that our batteries run low, and there is little charge left after awhile. No matter how critical the needs are, no matter how important the work is that we do, we all need to go away to a quiet place and rest in God's simple presence. "Come to me, all you that are weary and are carrying heavy burdens, and I will give you rest. Take my yoke upon you, and learn from me; for I am gentle and humble in heart, and you will find rest for your souls. For my yoke is easy, and my burden is light" (Matthew 11:28–30).

Whether our resting is contemplative or verbal, outdoors or indoors, using the Bible or icons or a lovely garden or a blank wall in front of us, we must all find ways of coming to God when we are weary and burdened. As Thomas Merton said, "Prayer is wasting time conscientiously with God." Wasting time—even with God—is difficult for us in our purpose-driven society. But taking time for intentional quiet and prayer is critical. For in doing so, we return to the understanding that simply being alive is a good and noble thing. We remember that there is a powerful divine source of peace and vitality, like a deep spring of fresh water that lies beneath the surface of all our superficial and anxious activity. If Jesus himself had to take time to return to the source, and he lived in a relatively much slower, quieter and nature-oriented time than we do, how much more we need to do the same, in our frantic modern world.

We remember that it is possible to "gain the whole world, but lose ourselves" (Luke 9:25). Like the rich fool who spent his life working and accumulating riches, only to die anyway with a full storehouse and an empty heart, "so it is with those who store up treasures for themselves but are not rich toward God" (Luke 12:21). Instead, we are to drop our worries as we are able, come to God, celebrate the wonder and beauty of life like a bird, a lily, like the grass of the field, and "strive for this kingdom. . . . for where your treasure is, there your heart will be also" (Luke 12:31, 34).

But whether our prayer is a spontaneous response to everyday life or intentional time that we take to be with God, it is to be heartfelt and trusting. Like a child, Jesus prayed to God as *Abba*. It is a measure of our reluctance to really embrace this kind of intimacy with God that the Church has translated Abba as "Father." More accurately, it means "Daddy," "Papa." In fact, I believe that Jesus' loving intimacy with Daddy-God was part of what got him crucified. To claim such closeness with the eternal Creator of heaven and earth: why this was blasphemy!

But claim it he did. Turning to Daddy-God (or Mommy-God, if you prefer), Jesus looked to him/her as a child to its loving parent: with affection and in complete confidence. Ask what you will and trust. For if you, imperfect and human as you are, lovingly give to your children what they need and desire, so much more will God give the same to you (Matthew 7:9–11).

Whether we are experienced contemplatives or new at prayer, illiterate or highly educated, this principle holds true. We are all beginners before God. We are all children before a loving Abba, needing, trusting, hoping. "Truly I tell you, whoever does not receive the kingdom of God as a little child will never enter it" (Mark 10:15).

Every time I think I know what I'm doing spiritually, I am humbled and realize once again I know nothing. Every time I think I know how to pray, my expertise shatters into a jumbled mess, and I can only plead for help. Either because I've entered into a stressful phase of my life or just because I've become complacent, my contemplation, for instance, turns to a crowded whirl of confusion. I get no peace. I become a beginner again, a spiritual know-nothing. All I can do is drop my trained "ability" to pray at this point and ask for God to pray through me.

After all, if prayer is only a matter of gaining expertise, then it is all about me, isn't it? My skill, my discipline, my ability to stay centered. We do learn about prayer from experience, of course, but we will always remain dependent upon God's grace in prayer, like a beginner, like a child. With this humility, we know that whatever happens in prayer is God's doing, not ours. The loving grace of God is what matters in prayer.

As beginners, as humble children in prayer, we must also learn to drop our insistence that we have a predictable experience when we pray. We must learn to forget about expectations entirely and just pray, simply, humbly, trustingly: Lord, I cannot reach you. But I do not ask that I may be able to feel you now; I only ask that you work in the hidden world of my heart.

Wonderful, peaceful and powerful experiences do happen in prayer, from time to time. But when they do, we might recall what a Zen teacher said to me: "It's not how high you can jump in meditation, but what you do when you hit the ground." Peter, James and John had a powerful experience on the Mount of Transfiguration with Jesus (Mark 9). They saw him gleaming with the brightness of divinity. Peter wanted to hold onto this moment, insisting that they build some tents on the spot and remain there. Instead, Jesus headed them back down the mountain, telling them to remain silent about it, as they headed toward the reality of his suffering and cross.

When the Pharisees came to argue with Jesus, they asked him for a "sign from heaven." We can feel Jesus' weariness with this type of spirituality as "he sighed deeply in his spirit and said, 'Why does this generation ask for a sign? Truly I tell you, no sign will be given to this generation'" (Mark 8:11–12).

It is hard to continue in prayer if we are expecting signs and rewards for having prayed. Forever wanting God to give us a feeling that we have predetermined to be the sign of divine presence (peace, warmth, calmness, joy, clarity of mind), we will forever be disappointed. Having made an unconscious bargain with God that we will put in our time in prayer if God will give us wonderful experiences, we discover that God never made such a deal with us. Instead, Jesus asks us to stand before God simply, directly, trustingly like a child, and not look for signs.

We speak of a "good" period of prayer or meditation. We complain about how we're "not getting anything out of prayer." Who are we to judge the quality of our prayer, to assume that we know what constitutes an authentic encounter with God? How do we know what is happening in the hidden world of our heart? How do we know how God is silently acting within us?

It is often only in hindsight that we can see God's response to our prayer. It is only by looking back over time that we see God's action in our lives. We pray, we ask for grace, we don't necessarily feel it in the moment, but all the while God is at work. Later on, we find that we have been given more patience, more trust, more love for others.

Finally, Jesus' prayer was one that was clearly shaped by the faith community of which he was a part. His was not an individualized, private spirituality of his own construction. He knew the scriptures, he followed Jewish law, and he attended traditional worship in his faith community. He "went to the synagogue on the sabbath day, as was his custom" (Luke 4:16). Jesus' parents raised him in a religious tradition, and he continued as an adult to observe the prescribed feasts, fasts, sacrifices, and pilgrimages to Jerusalem. As Jesus said, "Do not think I have come to abolish the law or the prophets; I have come not to abolish but to fulfill" (Matthew 5:17). That is to say, he came not to invent a privatized spirituality of his own; he came to bring the potential of traditional Jewish religious practices to creative fulfillment.

Jesus' personal life of prayer was no doubt shaped by his

tradition. Ours is too. As we receive the sacraments, study the Bible, and gather as a community of faith, we absorb the theology and ethics of our tradition. We internalize and integrate the deep truths of the Incarnation, the Crucifixion, the love of God and the call to compassion, and we hope to become more fruitful, more balanced, and more healthy as a result. Without the wider context of our faith tradition's teachings, we run the danger of becoming limited, distorted, and self-centered in our privatized prayer. But as we pray in community for those in prison, for refugees and for the departed, as we name a wide range of sins and negligences in the Ash Wednesday liturgy, our view of both self and God expands.

Jesus may have only given one brief prayer as a specific teaching on how to pray. But by his life and by his many comments about prayer and faith, he communicated a great deal. In prayer, we are to keep it simple and direct, personal and intimate. It is to be spontaneous, naturally arising out of the circumstances of everyday life, as we commute to work, as we remember a friend in trouble, as we watch the rain bless the earth with life.

Coupled with this, we are called to be intentional about taking time for prayer, temporarily leaving aside the cares of this life, so that we become rich toward God, storing up the treasure of truer and simpler things. Our daily time of prayer, if steeped in scripture or other spiritual writings, fills us up with insight and new perspectives that we would not otherwise gain.

So we always remain humble beginners, as children before God. Not expecting signs and wonders, we learn to trust that God is secretly at work, bringing to fulfillment whatever we need, no matter what our experience of prayer may be. And we are to be humble enough to need the breadth and wisdom of the traditional faith community, so that our prayer may be balanced and healthy.

wake up

When the early Christians wrote the gospels, they fully expected that Jesus would come again soon, physically, to complete his work in the world. Having been crucified and resurrected and ascended, they believed he was now going to come again in glory to judge and reign, to separate the sheep from the goats. At first, they thought it would happen in their lifetime. Later, they realized it might come later. It still hasn't happened.

And yet every week in the church we continue to recite this hope in the words of the Nicene Creed, the basic statement of our faith, when we say, "He will come again in glory to judge the living and the dead."

Are we deluded? Some think so. Others look up to the skies every time there is a significant historical convergence on the horizon, selling their possessions and waiting on a mountaintop with their fearless leader. Still others interpret the biblical teaching on "end times" by believing that someday, perhaps thousands or millions of years from now, the earth will have some kind of ending, just as it had a beginning. Nothing lasts forever.

Whatever your beliefs about a literal, historical second coming of Christ, there is no reason to throw out these readings as irrelevant simply because the events their authors foretold didn't happen as they imagined they would. There is also no reason to cling to them with one limited interpretation, as if they could have no other meaning than those intended by the original authors.

One of the powerful things about scripture is that it speaks on several different levels at once. Speaking specifically about God's protection of Israel from her military foes, the psalms also speak to us individually about God's loving care for us. Speaking specifically about a passionate, erotic love between a man and a woman, the Song of Solomon also speaks to us about a passionate, intimate relationship of love with God.

Whatever Jesus' disciples heard, remembered, and recorded in their dealings with Jesus, they wrote texts that eventually transcended their original intent. So without throwing out the original meaning of the text (which must always be taken into consideration), we can look at additional layers of meaning that these passages reveal. What layers are revealed when we look at what the gospel teaches about how we must remain ready for Jesus' coming?

In spirituality circles these days, there is much being written and taught about *mindfulness:* being present to the moment, appreciating the ordinary, slowing down and noticing the wonder of everyday life. This is one dimension of Jesus' teachings that is frequently overlooked. In the church's expectations about the second coming, we have often assumed that where Jesus says, "Be alert," he is speaking only about the end times. Not necessarily.

In Matthew 25, Jesus said that "the kingdom of heaven will be like this." Then he told a story of ten bridesmaids who waited for the bridegroom to arrive for a wedding. Five of the bridesmaids were foolish and five of them were wise. The foolish ones didn't prepare; they had no extra oil, they ran out, and they even became drowsy and fell asleep. The wise ones brought flasks of oil with them; they stayed awake. The foolish ones roused themselves from sleep, realized they were out of oil, and went off to buy some more. The bridegroom came in their absence, and only those who were wise were ready to go to the wedding. The foolish bridesmaids missed it completely. Finally, Jesus says to his audience, "Keep awake therefore, for you know neither the day nor the hour" (Matthew 25:13).

Now we can certainly understand this story in terms of the second coming of Christ. But we can also understand it as a parable about the spiritual life. Many of us live in a kind of dream existence. Shuffling off to work, driving the freeway, fixing a meal, fulfilling all our little duties, our minds are endlessly moving, worrying, imagining. We're not really present; we're asleep to life.

Mindfulness is the practice of waking up. Feeling our breath going in and out, looking at the sky, noticing the person in front of us, we awaken to the wonder of life itself, in this moment at hand. In his parables, Jesus frequently used the image of a wedding feast. His first miracle in the gospel of John was at a wedding feast in Cana. The wedding was a metaphor for our union with God, the coming together of the human and the divine in us. The kingdom of heaven was then the celebration of this loving union: God is in and among us— in fact all of life is filled with God—and this is something we should wake up to, so that we can live in joy and wonder.

God does come at unexpected times. The predictable moments are easy: sunsets, births of babies, passion between lovers, a warm evening with friends. But God's presence "in the moment" is not limited to these times. God is also fully present in our difficulties, in our loneliness, in our pain. Are we alert enough to notice the wedding feast here, too? Can we feel both the pain and the richness of life at once? Can we awaken to God's presence in this kind of "unexpected hour"? God is coming when we least expect it, not just in the sunsets and the warmth of love. God is coming when life is confusing, hard, and tedious.

Being awake is not always pleasant. Being awake sometimes means that we open ourselves to the fullness of the moment when we'd rather not. But the amazing thing is that when we do, the moment, even if difficult, expands to become something more than just "difficult." It also becomes wondrous, in its own way: wondrous in the sense of its depth, its richness, its pathos, wondrous as a beautiful requiem mass or tragic opera.

Mindfulness is the practice of staying awake no matter what is going on. It is the choice to remain present, rather than checking out. It is the act of opening to all of life. Like the wise bridesmaids, we stay in the moment, with our lamps lit, keeping awake, not going off into distractions, watching for the coming of God.

But there is another sense in which the gospels call us to remain alert. We are to choose God this day, to live as God intends us to live this day, and not wait for tomorrow to do so. For tomorrow, we may die.

Early Christians were well aware of this fact. Life could be brutal and short, especially for those being actively hunted down and persecuted, as they were. In this context, we feel the urgency of these words: "Be alert at all times, praying that you may have the strength to escape all these things that will take place, and to stand before the Son of Man" (Luke 21:36). "Be dressed for action and have your lamps lit" (Luke 12:35).

We may not live in danger most of the time, but our lives are still relatively short. How do you want to live? When will you start living this way? Many years ago as a young adult, I went through a crisis in my life that shook me to my core. One night I ended up imagining myself as an old man on my deathbed. I pictured myself thinking about my life, now over. I looked over my life and asked myself, What did I give myself to? In that moment, I gave myself to God. I dedicated my life to the pursuit of a holy life. I had no idea at that time that I would end up in the ordained ministry; that's not what this moment was about. It was about choosing to live into the promises of faith. I wanted to know through my own experience what Jesus was talking about. I wanted to live in freedom, joy, love, and harmony.

How do you want to live? I still ask myself this question frequently. I ask it when I find myself drawn into distraction and attachment, into ambition and fear. I ask it when I find myself caught up in something that does not lead to God. Asking the question, I am challenged to choose. Choosing God, I wake up again as if from a dream. I reenter life as it is intended to be.

In medieval times, people often waited until their deathbed to be baptized. This was a risky gamble, for it assumed that one could live however one wanted to—perhaps in dissipation, exploitation of others, and selfishness—and as long as you didn't die unexpectedly, it could all be made better at the end with absolution, baptism and last rites. The best of both worlds! You can have it all! Give yourself to a life of debauchery and go to heaven, too!

Now most of us don't approach the faith in this way anymore, but we do put off the choice for God. We vaguely assume that someday, perhaps, when we've got more time or less stress, we'll really devote ourselves to God. Then we'll get it together and live the way we know we're created to be.

Jesus' words should haunt us:

> But understand this: if the owner of the house had known in what part of the night the thief was coming, he would have stayed awake and would not have let his house be broken into. (Matthew 24:43)

> Therefore, keep awake—for you do not know when the master of the house will come, in the evening, or at midnight, or at cockcrow, or at dawn. (Mark 13:35)

> Keep awake therefore, for you know neither the day nor the hour. (Matthew 25:13)

And what I say to you I say to all: Keep awake. (Mark
13:37)

It's not that we must be always looking over our shoulders, in case God, the angry judge, might catch us doing
something we know we shouldn't be doing. It's that when we
live in a dream world, when we go through life half awake,
when we give ourselves over to things that only leave us
empty in the end, we are missing out on life. We are missing
out on the wonder and joy of the kingdom of heaven. We are
like the foolish bridesmaids or the sleeping owner of the
house, and life is passing us by.

Now is always the time to choose God. *Now* is always the
time to rouse yourself from sleep, look around you, and be
grateful for life. *Now* is always the time to begin to live.

27

you have to
serve somebody

On his 1979 album *Slow Train Coming*, when he was writing overtly Christian songs, Bob Dylan sang:

> *You're gonna have to serve somebody,*
> *It may be the devil or it may be the Lord*
> *But you're gonna have to serve somebody.*

We may think of ourselves as free and independent. Americans in particular like to think so. We pride ourselves on our individualism. Ironically, those who do so the most loudly seem to conform themselves to one of the "alternative" groups in fashion: rugged cowboy, punk rocker, struggling artist, tree-hugger, anti-Hollywood moralist.

More seriously, we are less independent than we think in our deepest values. Having been brought up in and fully immersed in any given culture, we take on at least some of its assumptions. Like most of those around us, we run around in cars, spend ourselves into debt, attend self-consciously to our appearance, glibly justify wars of intervention, consume hours in front of an electronic monitor, and parrot back the slogans of public figures filtered through the media as if they were self-evident truths about life. All the while we think we are independent.

Years ago my family and I were traveling in the South Pacific. On a boat one day, skirting closely along several small islands, my sons and I leaned over the railing, watching the residents go about their daily business. They were poor, but seemed to have everything they needed. Some were picking fruit, tending gardens or fishing in the sea, pigs were roaming around, small fires were burning, children were playing and old folks sat around talking. My sons and I began talking about where and how we live: malls, asphalt, television news and sitcoms, public dramas of the famous, endless bills to pay, email to keep up with, consumer choices defined and limited by corporate marketing, dense automobile traffic, and a crowded calendar day and night. All of a sudden one of my sons said, "We live such a bizarre life!"

Contrasting with the way the rest of the world lives, those of us in the modern industrialized world do indeed have a bizarre life. And yet we think of it as normal. I'm not saying that it is wrong to live the way we do or that other cultures are spiritually and morally superior; I'm just stepping back and looking at how we give ourselves completely over to what we have come to believe is normal.

We serve cultural values and norms without thinking about it. We may think we have no choice (which makes us more of a slave than a servant), but still, we serve somebody. As humans we live in community. None of us stands alone, completely free to think and do exactly as we please. Our thoughts, values, needs, even the realistic options of what we may and may not do are shaped by the world around us. One may have been a fourth-century Christian hermit in North Africa, a mother in medieval Europe, a poor Colombian farmer today,

> *You may be a state trooper, you may be a young Turk,*
> *You may be the head of some big TV network,*
> *You may be rich or poor, you may be blind or lame*
> *You may be living in another country under another name,*
> *But you're gonna have to serve somebody. (Dylan, again)*

We all serve at least some of the assumptions and values of our time and place in history. Jesus was certainly a man of his time, fully human like the rest of us. As a devout Jew, a working-class craftsman, a man in a traditionally patriarchal society, he wore the cultural blinders of his time, to some degree. As an example, he didn't know about psychiatric diagnoses, and so he probably believed, along with everyone else in his day, that certain maladies were demonic in nature.

In one remarkable story, we witness Jesus being liberated from one of his social limitations when a Syrophoenician (therefore Gentile) woman confronted Jesus' cultural prejudices as a Jew.

> She begged him to cast the demon out of her daughter. He said to her, "Let the children be fed first, for it is not fair to take the children's food and throw it to the dogs." But she answered him, "Sir, even the dogs under the table eat the children's crumbs." Then he said to her, "For saying that, you may go—the demon has left your daughter." (Mark 7:26–29)

This passage is often interpreted by preachers as a story in which Jesus was "testing" this woman's faith by initially refusing her request. After all, we couldn't have the divine Christ ever behaving in a rude or exclusive manner. More likely, it is a story about this very human Jewish rabbi being forced to come to terms with the liberating, radical scope of God's call on him: to reach out beyond Jewish purity laws, even to Gentiles. In this encounter, Jesus was confronted by a Gentile woman, his blinders fell off, and he grew more fully into his calling as the one who would, as divine resurrected presence, transcend all cultural limitations. Eventually St. Paul would say that in Christ there is no distinction between Jew or Greek, male or female, slave or free person.

If in his lifetime, Jesus himself was influenced by the

values and beliefs of his time, then certainly we are as well. And yet Jesus was more free of them, and from this position of relative liberty spent much of his ministry challenging others to examine the kinds of things they served. Like money:

> No slave can serve two masters; for a slave will either hate the one and love the other, or be devoted to the one and despise the other. You cannot serve God and wealth.
> (Luke 16:13)

This warning is as fresh today as it was two thousand years ago. The temptation of the material world is an eternal siren, luring us on to the rocks of ruin. This is not just a matter of concern for those who are obviously materialistic, greedy, and superficial. We are all consumers, we all worry about having what we want and need. John D. Rockefeller was asked, "How much money is enough?" And he answered, "Just a little more." And consumerism is not the only thing we serve. We serve popularity, power, success, the comforts of food and alcohol, our self-image as a good person.

The problem with servitude to anything other than God is that it will never deliver on its promise. Lesser gods lead us magnetically into a vacuum, where the pursuit only makes us hungry for more. As Frederick Buechner said, "Lust is a thirsty man eating salt in the desert." It doesn't deliver its falsely promised love and affection, which we so genuinely crave. Seeking constant approval from others, we will never get enough, and we will harm ourselves and others in the effort. Seeking the ecstasy of self-transcendence in drugs or alcohol, it will eventually deaden us to life. Seeking security, we will become fearful, even paranoid.

This is the foundation of idolatry: living in servitude to something that will never deliver what it promises. The very first commandment given to the people of Israel by God (who reminded them as he gave them this law that he had just recently brought them out of slavery) is, "You shall have no other Gods before me" (Exodus 20:3). Throughout the Hebrew scriptures, the Jews fall in and out of servitude to false gods, and God calls them whores and adulterers for doing so. God comes across as a jealous lover, demanding faithfulness.

Notice in this biblical metaphor, notice in Jesus' own teachings, that there is an assumption that we will serve *somebody*. In fact, references to servants and slaves abound in the gospels. Some serve money, Roman soldiers, temple officials, or rich landlords. In contrast to these forms of servitude, Jesus does not say that his followers are to be free and independent. They are to serve God, the poor, one another, the kingdom of God. They are to be good and faithful servants of the master of the kingdom of God. You've got to serve somebody. There is no such thing as complete independence. We are interdependent, interconnected as one body to the earth, to all people everywhere, to God. Either we serve those connections that lead to life, peace, justice, love, and harmony, or we serve something else.

What does it mean for us to serve God? It would be easy enough to assume that if we worship and pray regularly, if we believe the traditional doctrines and follow the moral guidance of the church, then we are, in fact, serving God. There is no such assumption in the gospels. To a shocked audience of pious but presumptive Jews, John the Baptist said, "Do not begin to say to yourselves, 'We have Abraham as our ancestor'; for I tell you, God is able from these stones to raise up children to Abraham" (Luke 3:8b). In an even more disturbing passage, Jesus spoke of those who would be shut out of the kingdom of God, even though they assumed that they knew and served God. They claimed, "'We ate and drank with you, and you taught in our streets.' But [the owner of the house, God] will say, 'I do not know where you come from; go away from me, all you evildoers!'" (Luke 13:26–27).

We serve God when we love, when we care for the marginalized. We serve God when we live in such a way that brings clarity of mind, emotional balance, and a healthy body. We serve God when we seek reconciliation between ourselves and others with whom we are at enmity, and between our nation and others in the world. We serve God when we learn to avoid useless comforts and empty our hearts instead, so that there is room for God to quietly enter.

Whom and what do you serve? Do these things lead to life for you, for your loved ones, for those around you in need? Do they lead to God, do they lead to the quality of life God promises for all of us? We may all have to serve somebody, but it is never too late to change masters.

be yourself

many people seem to think that being a Christian involves becoming someone that they're not. They imagine someone who is always nice and hopeful, never filled with anger or lust or dark thoughts.

Unfortunately, we in the church have created this misperception. We've stressed certain kinds of predictable behavior over authenticity. We have allowed Christianity to be clothed with a particular cultural look and feel: pipe organ, nice clothes, Sunday manners for children, stained glass, polite conversation, hard-working committees, fiscal responsibility, deodorant and mouthwash!

What any of this has to do with Jesus or his gospel I will never understand, but it is the face of Christianity in our society. Consequently, many who do not fit this cultural straightjacket will never feel at home in the church: not because they are unable to relate to Jesus' teachings, but because they can't conform to the trappings with which we've covered the gospel.

When I went to seminary and in the first few years after ordination, a part of me feared that I had made a terrible decision to seek ordination in the church. I had grown up loving the liturgy of the church, but otherwise had never been very "churchy." No acolyting for me, no youth groups, and then when I was old enough to assert my own way, I lit out for venues that were more fun: the ocean, rock festivals, hitchhiking across the country, staying up all night with friends. In fact, I must say that until seminary, I found God primarily through music, wilderness, and by taking part fully in that brief period of ecstatic and innocent spirituality of the counter-cultural movement in the Bay Area and New England.

These "secular" forms of what were, for me, a very real spiritual awakening eventually led me back to the church, where I pictured myself as a future priest who would be fully immersed in a life of prayer, service, worship, community, and the liberating power of Jesus' teachings. Imagine my surprise when it began to dawn on me that perhaps my future would be dictated more by potlucks rather than prayer, polite chats over cookies and coffee rather than deep conversations about faith, board meetings rather than direct service to the poor, and the fierce determination that nothing too creative, too challenging, too messy or too *human* would embarrass this pious gathering of God's Good People.

Yet I found that church can be a place of remarkable authenticity, a place of deep prayer and meditation, genuine conversation about things that matter, intelligent examination of our lives in light of the gospel, and meaningful service to a hurting world.

The difference between a culturally-bound church and an authentic one has to do with whether the people are being encouraged to be themselves, to be real. Where there is superficial cultural conformity, there is no room for humans to be who they are, to question the norms, to doubt, to bring the messiness of their lives into the room. They must, at all costs, retain the proper image.

By contrast, the authentic church encourages messiness; it welcomes people who aren't holding it all together for the sake of appearances; it hopes that some will question the basics; it does not shrink back from imperfection and failure; it doesn't fear strong emotion or lack of control. Besides, isn't that what Jesus modeled for us?

No matter who he was dealing with, Jesus was concerned with one thing, and one thing only: a transformation of the heart to God, so that the believer might be more loving and more free. Social status, religious trappings, even expected behavior were all secondary to this one vision. What mattered to Jesus was an authentically human life, grounded fully in the Spirit.

So the question really is, Where is holiness to be found? Is it in appearances, or in a truly Jesus-like quality of the heart? Is it in church or is it in life? If God's holiness is to be found in life itself, then it is when we are fully human, fully real, fully ourselves that we find the real God. It is in our struggles to be loving and true, to move beyond resentment and fear, to awaken to the wonder of life that God becomes real for us and for others around us.

Each of us is created uniquely, with very personal characteristics. We are created this way by our Creator, in whose image we were made. Each of us—as we are, not as we think we should be—is made to reflect a tiny part of the infinitely vast nature of God. When we are most ourselves then we most accurately reflect the glory of God. As St. Irenaeus of the second century put it, "The glory of God is the human person fully alive."

Jesus was fully alive, fully himself: so much so that he frequently shocked people around him with his words and his behavior. He didn't fit the stereotype of a religious teacher. He didn't conform to external expectations. Rather, he listened deeply to the voice of the Spirit within and acted accordingly.

What this takes is genuine trust in God. Of course we must listen to the wisdom of religious tradition; we do not stand alone, marching only to the sound of our own personal drumbeat. Individualism can lead us into some strange, isolated, small, and unhealthy areas if we are unwilling to subject ourselves to a community and a tradition that is bigger and wiser than we are personally. But given this listening, this willingness to be accountable to something larger than the self, we must then be free to move around within it in our own way. Casting off unnecessary trappings that have nothing to do with the gospel itself, we must listen deeply to the ways in which God moves and inspires us individually.

Do you feel God most directly when you sing the blues? Then sing the blues and call it prayer. Do you blurt out things that everyone seems to be thinking but no one is saying? Blurt on, and call it the prompting of the Spirit. Do you love to cook and eat? Hold parties and consider it Holy Communion. Do you like to keep things neat and orderly? Count the church's money on Sundays after services and remember that this, too, is service to God.

Jesus was very clear about this. As humans, we are salty, filled with unique flavors; we shine forth a particular quality of divine light. Don't suppress these divine gifts, he said:

> You are the salt of the earth; but if salt has lost its taste, how can its saltiness be restored? It is no longer good for anything, but is thrown out and trampled under foot.
>
> You are the light of the world. A city built on a hill cannot be hid. No one after lighting a lamp puts it under the bushel basket, but on the lampstand, and it gives light to all in the house. In the same way, let your light shine before others, so that they may see your good works and give glory to your Father in heaven. (Matthew 5:13–16)

Be yourself. For by seeing you as you really are, by seeing your light, others will see in you the One who is the source of your light. By keeping your saltiness, others will taste the Spirit as it moves through your life. And then they, too, will know that the only place they will ever find God is in the authenticity of *their own* life experience.

die to yourself

We all know someone with the Martyr Complex: someone who serves her own ego by appearing to be selfless. Such people are tirelessly cooking, cleaning, visiting those in the hospital, giving presents, calling others on the telephone, serving as a volunteer on endless committees. Meanwhile, their heart becomes hardened. Highly aware of their own efforts to be good, they resent others who do not act likewise. Shoving into the unconscious all the little disappointments they've suffered and the injustices they've absorbed, their anger boils beneath the surface. They become a kind of doormat that bites.

This is not Christian self-denial. It is an unhealthy, superficial caricature of true spiritual self-denial. Unfortunately, this caricature has been promoted by the church so that it might better dominate its members. We have been told that we must carry our cross, which we're told means that we must do what those in authority tell us to do, and put aside any questions we may have about it. Women in particular have suffered from this twisting of the gospel. They have been expected to put aside their own dreams and needs, serving their families and their church at all times. Fortunately, this is changing.

There is a healthier form of self-denial that Jesus taught. Calling his disciples to self-denial, he modeled it by the way he lived and died, eventually being willing to die for others.

Jesus asked his disciples to give up their money, their time, their very lives, if need be. He called them to forget their little grievances and petty sense of deserving and open their eyes to the needs of others around them.

Perhaps the most stark statement along these lines is when he said, "If any want to become my followers, let them deny themselves and take up their cross daily and follow me" (Luke 9:23). Note that he speaks of taking up a cross daily; this is to be an everyday practice, not some heroic thing we do once in our life. It is to be a lifestyle. What can this mean?

When we develop as children, it is natural and critical for us to build a healthy ego. We can't live without boundaries and the ability to value ourselves. After all, to deny oneself, one first has to have a self to deny.

But the healthy development of an ego is a far cry from a life lived in service of it. Self-denial begins when we start to notice the habitual ways in which we live only for ourselves: our anxiety about pleasing others, our tendency to make sure we get what we want before others have a chance to take it from us, our efforts to promote our intelligence, experience, and wisdom. Noticing the ego at work, bringing it under the light of awareness, we then are in a better position to make a choice against it in the future. When we have brought the habits of the ego-self into the light of awareness, we are then more likely to catch it in the moment that it next comes into play, and decide not to let it happen. What happens then?

Like someone who decides to fast from food for a period of time, there is an empty space that we will have to tolerate. Instead of advantage that comes when we strive for position, we are left on an equal plane with everyone else. Instead of the smiles of others that come in response to our codependency, we are left with a neutral or even hostile gaze. Instead of arranging things so that we get exactly what we want, we must do with what comes to us.

We must then tolerate this new sensation, this empty

feeling. Tolerating it, we eventually discover that it will not kill us. In fact, it leads us to a new and unexpected way of being that brings life in unexpected ways. Life that is not in service of the ego is actually just fine, the way it is! It's even fuller, more free, because it isn't twisted up in the little knots of our complicated emotional life. Life can be just what it is, which is often pretty wondrous and beautiful.

This is a form of self-denial. It is a kind of crucifixion of the ego-self. As we nail our habitual self-serving behavior to the cross, it eventually dies. And in dying, we are born again to a new way of being. We are resurrected.

Another way of denying ourselves and taking up our cross is in less psychological, more practical, and even dramatic ways: the soldier who puts others' lives ahead of his own, dying in service to country; the mother who gets up at 3 a.m. for the fourth time in the night, nursing a baby to sleep; the parent who sacrifices time and energy in order to put a child through college; the public servant who goes to yet another neighborhood meeting to listen patiently to people's concerns; the youth who denies the pressure of friends and does the right thing.

And so self-denial is often an action. In our society, we may not be called upon to lay down our lives as martyrs literally, but we will be called upon to sacrifice something in the service of the greater good. How do we muster up the will to do this? Paradoxically, the capacity to deny the self must also come from a developed sense of self. It is only the person who is secure in their own ego who can lay that ego aside in order to serve the greater good.

Jesus said deny yourself; take up your cross; follow me to Calvary. Where is this call in your life today? Is it in denial of the ego, in fasting from habits of self-centered living? Or is it in self-sacrifice, in dying a bit so that others might live more fully? Either way, your crucifixion will not only benefit others around you; it will result in your own resurrection as well.

keep the faith

J esus promised us hope, even when things are very dark:

> Blessed are you who are poor, for yours is the kingdom
> of God.
> Blessed are you who are hungry now, for you will be
> filled.
> Blessed are you who weep now, for you will laugh.
> Blessed are you when people hate you, and when they
> exclude you,
> revile you, and defame you on account of the Son of Man.
> Rejoice in that day and leap for joy, for surely your re-
> ward is great in heaven; for that is what their ancestors
> did to the prophets. (Luke 6:20–23)

What sense does this really make? In *this* world and in *my*
life, where is this kingdom, this inheritance of the kingdom, this
blessing when we mourn and are hated and are poverty-
stricken? Just look around. The world is a mess, the greedy and
powerful and wicked are rewarded, and there is no end in sight
for the misery of the downtrodden. And our own personal
troubles are certainly not magically whisked away when we try
to place our trust in the Lord.

Once I went to a conference in Birmingham, Alabama.
The highlight of the trip for me had nothing to do with the

conference itself. It took place during a rainy walk in Ingram Park, where many of the civil rights marches of Birmingham originated, where Martin Luther King and many other leaders spoke beatitudes to other troubled and poor masses who pressed upon them. Across the street is the 16th St. Baptist Church, where four girls attending church were killed by a firebomb.

The park features a kind of civil rights Stations of the Cross (without calling it that), with statues of children being brutally firehosed, arrested, and set upon by police dogs. The ghost of Bull Connor, the cruel sheriff who lead the attacks on demonstrators, comes alive when you walk a narrow sidewalk sculpture, where four vicious German shepherds, sharp teeth bared, lunge toward you out of close high walls on either side. As I walked the stations, I found my pace slowing down, my mind struggling to comprehend what I saw, and my heart broken.

The Civil Rights Institute, just off the park, was a revelation. Photographs and films show bombings, beatings, lynchings, and venomous hatred being hurled at children who were just trying to go to school. They also display the quiet, courageous, nonviolent witness of those remarkable martyrs of the faith, who proclaimed the gospel of hope in this darkness: Blessed are the poor, the hungry, those who weep, and those who are hated, reviled, excluded and defamed on account of the Son of Man. Your reward will be great, for that is what their ancestors did to the prophets.

When I was a young adolescent, I saw this remarkable chapter in history unfolding in the news, and ever since, I have read about it, watched films and photographs, heard speeches, and seen legislation argued over and passed. But being there was a whole other matter. It was as if the wind had been knocked out of me. It was a powerful experience of knowing, suddenly, *This really happened. Here. In this place. These people gave their lives for the gospel.*

And there, at the entrance to the park is a statue of Martin

Luther King, with a remarkable inscription below his likeness: "His dream liberated Birmingham from itself and began a new day of love, mutual respect, and cooperation."

When I saw this I was overwhelmed with the realization that while there is still racism and injustice, at this time in Birmingham and elsewhere the blacks of the civil rights movement—those very people who were hated and scorned and excluded—have become the heroes, the victors. The racists—those who at one time held all the power—were humbled. God was victorious.

In God's time, by grace and by untiring and courageous work, the poor are lifted up and the mighty are brought down from their thrones. The mournful rejoice, the righteous prosper, the hungry are filled, the dead are raised up. But woe to those who were rich, full, and laughing. Woe to the wicked, for their way is doomed.

It is important to remember history, for as people of faith, we take the long view. We live in remembrance of our Jewish and Christian heritage, our ancient message of hope proclaimed by the prophets, as it slowly influences humanity, at God's own pace. We recall how the Spirit works over time. We must think about how far humanity has come, in so many ways. As Mahatma Gandhi said when things in India looked particularly bleak for his movement, "Don't you know that good always eventually wins, that tyrants always fall?"

All of this recollection is important, for it releases us from the prison of current circumstances. Watching the news now in 2004, as I am writing this, it would be easy to assume that life is determined by terrorist threats, weapons of mass destruction, and anxious attempts to ensure our security. While these are important concerns of our day, they are not all there is. The historical faith perspective also helps us see the bigger picture: that life is good, God is involved, and everything will come out all right in the end.

There are many places in life now that need this kind of

confidence and trust. You know what they are. Some of us are terribly alarmed by the trend toward preemptive wars, the influence of global corporations, and the erosion of civil rights. Gay and lesbian people today are scapegoated as the unclean among us, wildly accused of choosing a morally repugnant lifestyle that they neither, in fact, ever chose or actually live. Homeless families inhabit our streets, and millions go without clean water or medical care. In our own personal lives, we may struggle with depression, illness, economic uncertainty or divorce.

We need hope. But what kind? A hope that is based upon current politics and today's headlines will fail us. A hope that is based upon how things are going for us personally right now may well disappoint us. Our hope must be based upon the longer view, the evolution of humankind, and the slow but inexorable power of God working among us.

Yet we must also not passively wait for these things to come magically into being by the hand of God. We must not passively wander through this land of sorrow until we receive our reward in the sweet bye and bye. Gandhi said that "passivity is worse than violence because it strengthens the evil it ignores." We must strive with God toward the justice which we trust will inevitably come to pass.

And so by our efforts and by the persistent force of goodness itself, I have confidence that liberty and human rights will continue to slowly spread in this world, and that the tyrannical ways of violence and oppression are ultimately doomed. I believe that we will eventually pay decent wages for hard work, feed the hungry and care for the vulnerable ones among us who are sick and mentally ill. I know that we will gradually get over our irrational prejudices toward gay and lesbian people and all minority "others." I trust that someday enough of us will want peace and cooperative harmony among the nations more than we want our selfish privileges and advantages over one another.

As people of faith we look for resurrection as the inevitable direction and fulfillment of all creation, including our society, our church and our personal lives. As Martin Luther King said, "The arc of the moral universe is long, but it bends toward justice." And so we strive with God to push the world ahead, beyond this death into new life. We are patient, steadfast, inching our way forward, by God's grace, into the kingdom of heaven.

This is what the civil rights workers did. They kept their eyes on the prize. Their hearts were set upon the gospel hope of redemption, in spite of their temporary setbacks and losses. They knew God was on their side, and that ultimately God would not disappointment them. God is on the side of those who suffer, those who mourn now and are hated and unjustly reviled. God is with the righteous, even when the world is not.

So keep the faith. Strive toward the kingdom. Do not fear. Blessed are all of us who trust in the Lord.

31

be contemplative

J esus is many things to many people. For some, he is a social activist. For others, he is a demanding moralist. Many
see him as a pal, easygoing and kind to everyone. Others still
envision him as a fully enlightened spiritual guru. Maybe he
was all of these things. Or perhaps all of us simply project on
to him anything and everything we want him to represent for
us. And so whether or not he actually was, I like to think of
Jesus as being contemplative at heart.

Now I know that Jesus didn't sit cross-legged all day long
in front of an icon, burning incense and emptying his mind.
But he displayed certain contemplative characteristics, which,
when remembered, have a way of encouraging those followers
of Jesus who happen to be oriented toward contemplation.

One of the stories that has illustrated this quality for contemplatives through the ages is the story of Martha and Mary
(Luke 10:38–42). Most of us are familiar with the story. Jesus
went to the home of his good friends Martha, Mary, and
Lazarus. We find him teaching and conversing with those who
were gathered around.

Martha was distracted with many tasks, cooking and
straightening up, attending to the needs of her guests. There
was much to do. Meanwhile, her sister Mary was just sitting
there, smiling, enjoying the company, listening to what Jesus
had to say. God knows where Lazarus was.

Martha's ire began to rise, and what did she do? Instead of

quietly taking her sister aside and asking her to please take part in the duties of hosting this party, she went to Jesus. She said to him, "Do you not care that my sister has left me to do all the work by myself? Tell her then to help me." Martha attempted to manipulate Jesus into taking sides against her sister. But Jesus responded, "Martha, Martha, you are worried and distracted about many things; there is need of only one thing. Mary has chosen the better part, which will not be taken away from her" (v. 40–41).

Mary had chosen the "better" part because she was taking the opportunity to listen to Jesus; she was engaged with him and others around him; she wasn't trying to make anyone else behave in this way or that. She was present to this unique and wonderful situation in her own way. Martha had chosen the "worse" part simply because she had lost her sense of presence. She seemed to care more about the food and the dishes and the seating order than the opportunity to be present to this remarkable moment.

What does this story tell us about Jesus' contemplative spirit? Simply this: that we must learn to stop, at times, and be present. We all know how tempting it can be to lose our ability to be present, because we get all caught up in things that seem necessary. Of course it would be nice to have a good meal prepared for Jesus and his friends. Of course it would be helpful to get the financial reports done in time for the meeting. Of course it would be good to clean up the yard when it's a mess.

But these activities have a way of becoming little tyrants over our mood, clouding everything, ruining the moment. Our minds become consumed with a list of things that must be accomplished, and we rush to get it done with a tight knot in our stomach because, well, *it must be done!* In our stress, we forget to look at the sky. We can't see the beauty of those around us whom we love. We miss the opportunity to make a joke, to appreciate the moment. Sometimes we are fortunate enough to have someone like Jesus around, who says, "Now,

now, why don't you drop all that for now and sit down here?"

This story teaches us to be really present and responsive to those moments in life that come along, which feed and nourish us. "Mary has chosen the better part, which will not be taken away from her." To stop our momentum, to pause and feel the goodness of life even for a moment, to really listen to another person: This is being fully alive. Doing this from time to time will have its cumulative effect upon us; it "will not be taken away" from us. We will become happier, more present to life, more appreciative of the small things.

This is really what contemplation is all about: learning to be present to the moment at hand. Whether or not one sits in the silence of contemplative prayer, we all need to learn how to stop our momentum and just be from time to time. It is in being that we leave behind the world of ambition and ego and worry for long enough to listen and watch for God's still, small voice. Thomas Merton's description bears repeating: "Prayer is wasting time conscientiously with God."

Jesus himself took time for just being with God. The region where Jesus reportedly went after his baptism in the Jordan River ("the wilderness" or "the desert") is especially evocative for contemplatives: rough, rocky soil, no hiding place, high mountains where one is exposed to sun and rain, violent robbers, and one's own inner, demonic voices. In the silence of this harsh contemplative landscape, he came to terms with Satan, he heard what God was asking of him now that he was baptized in the Spirit, and he found the resources to move with certainty where he was called.

Many passages of the gospels describe Jesus going off on a mountain, across the lake, to a "lonely place," in order to spend time, sometimes hours in solitary prayer. If you've ever gone to the region of Galilee in Israel, you can picture it. Rolling hills and mountains, secluded spaces, long vistas: This is a place where one can absorb the moment in God.

Jesus gave enough priority to time in these places even to

ignore, when necessary, the crying needs of those around him. At times he had to escape from the crowds, and even from his own disciples. One poignantly human passage describes Jesus' need for contemplative silence and his unwillingness to become captive to the demands of life:

> In the morning, while it was still very dark, he got up and went out to a deserted place, and there he prayed. And Simon and his companions hunted for him. When they found him, they said to him, "Everyone is searching for you." He answered, "Let us go on to the neighboring towns, so that I may proclaim the message there also; for that is what I came out to do." (Mark 1:35–38)

They hunted him down in his solitude in the early morning hours; they demanded that he go back to the last town they had visited, for some who had needs couldn't get to him because of the crowds; and he said no, we're moving on.

This last detail demonstrates another contemplative quality, and that is detachment. Jesus was not co-dependent, to put it in modern terms. He was not attached to pleasing everyone. He didn't heal everyone who needed healing. He would leave a situation, loose ends dangling all over, and go off to a deserted place in the dark and pray. Even when pressured to stay and help more, he might move on.

Contemplation teaches us about detachment. It doesn't remove the responsibility to love, but it places that responsibility within the context of a higher duty: to love God.

In contemplation, as was the case for Jesus, we feed the wellspring of our souls simply by loving God, by being present to the moment in the Spirit. Without "wasting time conscientiously with God," we will have nothing to give to others. Contemplation—finding spiritual nourishment in occasional solitude and silence—was for Jesus an absolutely necessary activity that restored his capacity to give.

turn, and live

a testy conversation with our next-door neighbor leads to guilt about what we've said. Another failed diet, and then shame. More time wasted in front of the television, and we worry that we are allowing life to pass us by. Anger at our children when we really knew they needed understanding. So we beat ourselves up, and we "repent," promising to be better people.

Take a different view: Jesus' call to repentance was not a condemnation of our nasty, evil nature. It was a plea for people to turn toward life. The love, joy, harmony, and peace which God desires and makes available is close at hand; it is never far away, never inaccessible. Jesus proclaimed, "Repent! For the kingdom of heaven has come near!" (Matthew 3:2) To paraphrase: Turn from those habits and patterns that keep you limited, unhappy and unloving—and re-orient yourself Godward, so that you can live into the divine life that is so close that it is already surrounding and inhabiting you.

What does it mean for us to do this? If repentance from sin is not a shameful feeling about our unworthiness, if it is instead a grace-filled turning from one way of life to another, how do we do it?

Self-help manuals and positive thinking authors advise us to make a plan, start small, develop new habits, and organize ourselves into a different person. This approach has its benefits, and it really seems to work to some degree. But the failure of diet plans, as one example, reveals the limitations of this course of action. Resolve and will power often only go so far before we find ourselves right back where we started, or worse, deeper in frustration because we've put in our best effort and still find ourselves stuck. Hope turns to despair.

The gospel approach to sin and repentance adds another dimension. It both recognizes our humanity and it invites us to more fully embrace our potential goodness. To the woman caught in adultery, Jesus forcefully showed her and others how the woman was really no more sinful than anyone else, and that no one was in a position to judge her. She was imperfect and had made mistakes, like all of us. In this acknowledgment of her and everyone's humanity, the woman was invited into new life; she was restored from alienation to community. In the story of the prodigal son, Jesus told how the prodigal "came to himself" and went home. As soon as the son saw what he had made of his life and then turned toward his home (toward God the Father), he was received with delight and love. No questions asked.

Jesus wanted us to understand that all we have to do is to turn to God without shame and desire the new life he offers. God then freely and joyfully offers us forgiveness. In Luke 12:32, Jesus said, "Do not be afraid, little flock, for it is your Father's good pleasure to give you the kingdom."

The dynamics of addiction and recovery illustrate this truth. An alcoholic—or for that matter, any of us who habitually gives ourselves over to anger or worry—suffers terribly from shame and constantly renewed intentions to be better. A closeted gay person agonizes over his or her "sin," and after every encounter promises God that it won't happen again. Coming to ourselves, we admit we're out of control in addiction, fear, or rage. We accept our sexual orientation as a given about our life. We admit who we are. We then turn to the God of love in hope that we might become more.

God can now work with us, when we become real. God responds to our turning with joyful grace: We are given the power to be sober, to let go of fear and anger, to live freely and responsibly with our sexuality as it is. All of this happens not because we beat ourselves up for being bad, but because we came to the truth, turned in hope to a gracious God, and then received what it is his good pleasure to give us.

It is divine forgiveness that adds a whole new dimension to our own process of healing as well. For while we may come to insight about the origins of our problems, and we can make efforts toward becoming a new person, without forgiveness—without a sense that we are fully accepted and affirmed just as we are and also invited to become more—change can be a dire, determined business filled with effort and self-evaluation. With acceptance and unconditional love, we can turn without shame and simply receive that which it is God's good pleasure to *give* to us.

The unconditional love of God is what provides the religious dimension to change, renewal, and healing. It is the dimension of *grace*: a power that transcends our own efforts and abilities. We turn toward life, and what we are met with in that turning is not a shaking finger: "I told you so!" Nor is it a difficult task to accomplish: "Now you've got your work cut out for you!"

Instead, when we turn away from sin and toward new life, we rejoin the flow of how we are designed to live, and a power enters into our lives and carries us along with it. We become animated by the divine from within, and this divine power does things in us we would never think of or be able to do on our own. It is God's good pleasure to give us the kingdom.

33

exercise your faith

Jesus was once approached by a man whose son was possessed by seizures. He said to Jesus, "'If you are able to do anything, have pity on us and help us.' Jesus said to him, 'If you are able!—All things can be done for the one who believes.' Immediately the father of the child cried out, 'I believe; help my unbelief!'" (Mark 9:22–24)

This short story is poignant for many of us who struggle to have faith. We see ourselves in the father. I believe . . . somewhat. But I also don't believe. I give some concern to God, only to take it back again in a day, attempting to control the outcome. With a similar mixture of faith and doubt, what does the father of the suffering child do? He doesn't slink away from Jesus, ashamed of his own lack of conviction. Instead, he puts himself forward anyway, asking for help to believe more fully.

I've been working on faith for many years now. I still don't fully trust that God will deliver. How do I know this? I still worry. Even though I know that, eventually, God will show me a way forward through any difficulty that life presents, even though I know that ultimately all of life and death is held in the love of God, I still worry. I worry about what will happen if there isn't enough money, or someone prevents me from getting what I want, or if the wrong person is elected or chosen for a position of authority over me. I do believe, I do have some measure of faith, but I also don't believe.

Jesus' response to this mixture of faith and doubt is not scorn or rejection, but acceptance. He healed the man's son. The man admitted the imperfection of his faith, and Jesus accepted what he was able to offer, without expecting perfection. He used the small amount of faith the man *did* have, and combined it with the power of his loving grace.

In another teaching, Jesus told us, "If you have faith the size of a mustard seed, you will say to this mountain, 'Move from here to there,' and it will move; and nothing will be impossible for you" (Matthew 17:20). Now this passage is often twisted into a formula for magic thinking: "If you make yourself believe hard enough and force out of your mind all doubt, you will get what you want."

In the name of this perverted theology, many have added spiritual shame to their already difficult circumstances. A child is very sick, and the parents begin to believe that she is not getting better simply because they don't "believe" hard enough. God is testing them, they think, and they are failing badly. But their faith or lack of faith is not something they can just decide to have; in a sense, it is out of their control. In their moment of need, like the father of the boy afflicted by seizures, they simply have whatever level of faith they have.

Instead, this parable about the mustard seed tells us that even if our faith is tiny, even if it is weak, we should employ it. Even if it is only the size of a small mustard seed, we should still use it to reach toward God. For faith must be activated—we can't wait for something to happen; we must employ whatever level of trust we have in God. How do we do this?

Certainly not by trying to make ourselves feel calm about something that troubles us, simply because we think we should present a faithful image to God. Instead, we hold out our trust toward God, saying, "Hey, it ain't much, but it's all I've got: I'm trying to count on you." Jesus tells us that God will honor even this small amount of trust. Why? Because answers to prayers do not come as a result of our perfect confidence; they come when our *attempt* to trust meets God's goodness. It is the attempt to have faith that matters.

Great things can happen with this attempt to exercise our faith. Mountains move. They move not because we are Giants of Faith, but because the mixture of our efforts to have faith and God's goodness results in a powerful chemistry. The ground moves, deep down like a quiet earthquake, and our very being is shaken at the roots. Mountains move when we risk the little bit of trust that we have.

When we do this once, it is easier the second time. When we discover that, in fact, God does respond when we call upon him, we are more likely to trust in this possibility in the future. Our faith grows. We learn by experience, not by convincing ourselves of some theological truth. I don't know anyone who learned to trust in God because a verse of the Bible told them they should. I know plenty of people who put their lives on the line, risking a kernel of truth the size of a mustard seed, and found out that God was there for them.

Often people come to my parish acting like scared rabbits. This is because they have in their history a very harmful experience with a church that was, in one way or another, abusive to them. It is a wonder they ever darken the door of a church again, but some little voice inside tells them that they still want and need God, worship, and community. They tiptoe in, ready to bolt at the slightest suggestion of a threat. But in their heart is a kind of courage, a tender willingness to risk their trust once again. Over time, as they realize they are in a safe environment, their heart opens to God, to worship, to other people. Their sense of God's presence in their life grows, their involvement in ministry increases, and they begin again to apply their faith to everyday circumstances. Mountains move.

Faith is the result of learned experience. If we were not fortunate enough to have been given early life experience that caused us to trust the world, we must create this experience. We create it by risking that it might be true. And because we are wary, we must do so in small doses. The size of mustard seeds. A little bit risked, a little bit gained. Soon we will learn through experience, and eventually we will give the whole thing up in trust, and mountains will move.

forgive yourself
for being human

There is such a thing as good guilt. If we've been mean to someone just because they pushed our buttons, if we strike our children in anger, if we betray our beloved partner with a lie, then naturally we feel guilty. Hopefully, our conscience leads us to apologize and make amends for what we've done.

But then there is another kind of guilt, rooted in our own personal histories and religious upbringing. Voices of our parents echo in our brains, telling us that we're just not quite measuring up to expectations! We worry that we're too honest or too shy, too controlling or too uncontrollable, too nice or not loving enough. We carry all our faults and mistakes around like a dark, lurking cloud over our heads, highly aware of our unworthiness. Some Christian churches have, of course, instilled this kind of guilt, with their heavy emphasis upon our "sinful nature," as if we are permanently marked by the stain of original sin.

This guilt is really shame, a pervasive and vague sense that we're not as good as we ought to be. This is in spite of the fact that we know, rationally, that no one is perfect, and that the effort to try to be perfect only leads to neurosis, and that the origins of our emotional and behavioral imperfections began at a time when as innocent children we had no way of stopping patterns from being implanted permanently in our psyche.

As people of faith, what do we do, then, with a shameful feeling we have about ourselves from time to time? Some reject religion entirely, convinced that the whole enterprise is too steeped in guilt-inducement to do anything but harm; perhaps they work on building up their self-worth by assiduously affirming their goodness (a worthy effort for some, up to a point). But others of us cannot just wish away all sense of guilt. We must somehow learn to forgive ourselves for being human.

Jesus forgave sins. The gospels are filled with stories of absolution. He forgave those whom others were unwilling to forgive, not even waiting for them to repent first; he healed physical and psychic wounds by removing sin; he told parables about the gracious, abundant, unconditional love of God; and he even claimed the very power and authority to grant divine forgiveness. Everywhere he went, he accepted, loved, and healed the scars of guilt.

Of course, he called people to accountability, too. To the woman caught in adultery, he said, "Go your way, and from now on do not sin again" (John 8:11). But his basic stance toward others was an acceptance of human imperfection, not a condemnation of it. The man who was paralyzed and let down through a thatched roof, the many possessed by demons, the woman who wept as she washed his feet—with all of them, Jesus didn't dwell on their sin: he released them from shame by forgiving them. Jesus has compassion on our weakness, even as he invites us to take responsibility for our sin and change our life.

Accepting God's forgiveness for ourselves often begins with emotional and psychological insight. We come to understand the roots of our destructive patterns, and we see how they have played out in specific and general ways in our adult life. We finally admit how much anger we carry around, we realize we have a problem with compulsive overeating, or we discover how subtly we hide ourselves from being intimate with others. Often therapy or recovery groups contribute a great deal to this first step of awareness. We must understand how we were damaged by others or by unfortunate life circumstances before we can see why we continue to damage ourselves and others.

But insight and understanding don't necessarily free us. We still might live with regret for things we do and say, and for things we *fail* to do or say: "We have left undone those things we ought to have done, and we have done those things we ought not to have done, and there is no health in us," as the old confession put it. We still may carry around a list of shoulds, never quite living up to our own standards. We might still anxiously work at self-improvement, thinking that if we accomplish enough of it, then we'll be good.

It helps me simply to remember that I am human and always will be. Just like everyone else, I live somewhere on the continuum of brokenness and goodness, with some of us more sinful or holy than others, but all of us on it. I will never be perfect. I may grow in freedom and love, but I will always falter from time to time. My capacity for joy and wonder, my ability to serve others, my openness to God's loving guidance will always be limited, inconsistent. I continue to struggle to be emotionally honest with myself, to admit "dark" feelings, and I continue to worry and plan things so that I will get what I want. I am human.

Rather than this becoming a source of frustration and shame, can it be a source of relief? Can we drop our unrealistic expectations of perfection, and just be what we are? Can we continue to work toward continued insight, responsibility and self-improvement without falling into scrupulosity, basing our self-worth not on the accomplishment of these things but on God's delight in us as we are today?

We all know the ideal of a loving parent who does this for their child. Never releasing the sense of accountability that a mother has for her son, she always holds him in love. The son's imperfections are transparent to the mother, she always nudges him forward in growth toward maturity, but she never withdraws her complete acceptance. Her love is not conditional upon his self-improvement. She accepts him as he is, today.

If this is possible for some parents, surely it is possible for God. It is God's unconditional love that matters, not our worthiness. Of course we're not worthy of God, but that's not the issue. God simply loves us, and will always love us. Sometimes the remembrance of this can be such a relief. It allows us to "go home" to God, where we will always be taken in. Jesus' parable of the prodigal son makes this point powerfully (Luke 15:11–32). The son is ashamed of himself for having squandered his inheritance and his life. He imagines himself crawling home with his tail between his legs, but before he can deliver his well-rehearsed speech of confession, his father bursts forth with joy at the sight of his son, embraces him, orders a feast to be prepared, and exclaims, "Once you were lost; now you are found! Once you were dead, now you are alive!" (see v. 32)

Can you accept the fact of your humanity, and also the fact of God's love for you, in spite of your imperfection (or even because of it)? Can you just go home and return the embrace that God offers you today, as you are? This embrace is not based upon your repentance, your insight, or your firm dedication to change. It just is. It is simply offered to you as you are, today, without improvement. For we are not forgiven because we repent; we repent because we are forgiven.

Pray for the grace to accept God's embrace, daily if need be. Don't just confess your sins guiltily, in a way that will only more firmly entrench a sense of unworthiness. Admit your imperfections without shame or fear. Place all your trust in the One who loves you much more than you can ever love yourself. Just lay your humanness out there before a knowing God, who smiles and says, "Yes, this is true about you, isn't it? Now let's make some changes, and get on with life, shall we?"

do it now

a story is told about President Harry Truman, who was tired of advisors who spent too much time analyzing all the possibilities. He said, "What I need is a one-handed advisor!" Like Truman's advisors, many of us come to the edge of conviction, only to back slightly away, and say, "On the other hand. . . ."

In our psychological age which stresses ambiguity and understanding, we sometimes overlook one of the more striking and obvious qualities of the gospels: a clear decisiveness that Jesus both exhibits and expects of his followers. Fishermen who were called by Jesus to become his followers would just drop their nets and walk away from their livelihood. To those who delayed following him, Jesus said, "Let the dead bury their own dead. . . . No one who puts a hand to the plow and looks back is fit for the kingdom of God" (Luke 9:60, 62) Jesus demanded that the curious and rich young man commit himself by selling all his possessions and giving the money to the poor (Matthew 19:21–22).

Commit yourself. Follow me. Don't look back. Do something radical. Do it now.

Spiritual conviction and total commitment to God can be a difficult thing. Like religious tourists, we gaze at the landmarks of the kingdom of God as if we were outsiders. From a distance, we *see* the promises of hope, trust, unconditional love, and freedom from deadening habits. We *taste* these things from time to time. But we also hold back. For part of us enjoys being selfish, lazy, or even being worried all the time. They're familiar to us. We know how to navigate around our lack of love for other people, our occasional hopelessness, our domination of other people. The devil we know is better than the devil we don't know. Like those who commit crimes as soon as they get out of prison so that they can go back in to what has become a familiar environment, we fear freedom.

Once Jesus encountered a paralyzed man who for 38 years lay helplessly near the healing waters of the pool of Bethzatha, in Jerusalem (John 5:1–16). He complained that whenever the healing waters were stirred by the Spirit, no one would put him into the water, and someone else always got there first. When Jesus asked him, "Do you want to be made well?" it was not an idle question.

And yet, anyone who has ever tried to stick to a diet knows how hard it is to act with the kind of decisiveness these gospel passages suggest. Anyone who tries to take on a habit of daily prayer discovers something about their resistance to change. Any recovering alcoholic knows that will power alone will not result in successful recovery. At the gym I go to, every year in early January I see a troupe of out-of-shape men and women go through the introductory tour, and then appear regularly—for a little while.

So what is the point of spiritual decisiveness, if we are only going to fail? The fact is, the spirit is willing, but the flesh is weak. Knowing this, it is important to be careful about setting ourselves up for failure every time we decide that *this* time, we're *really* going to commit to God. Such resolutions are filled with willfulness, with grim determination, and they always fail. What is needed instead of willfulness is willingness.

Willingness is a state of readiness, an openhearted, active availability that patiently watches in hope for the possibility of change, and also watches for the obstacles that stand in the way of that change. With willingness, we pay close attention to the patterns of habit that keep us apart from holiness of life. We bring awareness to our attachments and compromises, and every time we do so, they wear thinner, they lose a little more of their power over us. Then, knowing we cannot affect real lasting change on our own, we must wait patiently for the moment of grace, when our willingness matches God's will and we are pushed forward by grace.

I grew up in the San Francisco Bay Area, and used to surf as a teenager. Sitting on a surfboard in the water, you must wait. You must be attentive, watchful, ready. When a swell comes along, you must apply your energy, paddling quickly with the wave. If you don't put in any effort, the wave passes you by and you go nowhere. But if you do point yourself in the right direction and paddle, and if it is the right moment, then the power of the wave—much stronger than your own weak paddling—matches your effort, picks you up, and carries you forward.

This is how our willingness can be utilized by the Spirit to affect real change. We cannot make ourselves holy, any more than surfers on a calm ocean can paddle themselves frenetically forward into a glorious ride. But we must be willing and attentive, or nothing will ever happen. With awareness, we wear down our resistance, our obstacles, our compromises. We attend to our desire for change, waiting watchfully, hopefully. Then when the healing waters are stirred by the Spirit, we must do whatever it takes to get ourselves into the water. When the wave begins to move us upward and forward, we must aim in the right direction and paddle.

The moment for decisiveness and conviction does come. Having waited attentively with a willing heart, at some point we reach a moment of clarity. In this moment, we know, without a doubt, that there is only one way forward that leads to life. If we step back from this moment, we become like the rich young man, skulking away sorrowfully, for we have knowingly denied an important chance offered by God (at least until it is offered again). But if we put our hand to the plow and don't look back, risking it all for the opportunity to be spiritually transformed, our decisive action is joined with God's intention for us.

There is a place for decisiveness. At times we must catch the wave, without hesitation. This moment of action does not come every day, and we can't force it willfully. But we can prepare for it, so that finally, when the heavy obstacles of our resistance have been worn thin, we become light enough for our determination to be raised up and carried forward by the divine movement of grace.

you can't do any of this

Home Depot holds very popular Saturday instructional workshops for the Average Jolene. Money-management gurus promise eventual wealth if we will consistently follow ten easy steps. They urge us to buy into an all-American characteristic that has been handed down to us from our Founding shopkeepers, homesteaders, and countless immigrants: "You can do it!"

And to a great extent, we can. It is amazing, in fact, what we can accomplish. Look at the Hoover Dam, the interstate highway system, the myriad advances in medicine and technology. I know a heart surgeon who grew up as a child in Vietnam during the horrors of that war, left her country with her parents on a flimsy overcrowded boat for the Philippines, emigrated to the United States, put herself through college and medical school, bought her parents a nice house, and now performs quadruple bypasses! How on earth did she do that?

And yet, not all of us can achieve such things through a can-do spirit alone. Most of us do not have the stamina for it. For every war-scarred boat person who triumphed as a heart surgeon, there are thousands who remain powerless over their situation and paralyzed by their pain. Besides, I would guess that many of those who do triumph with a can-do spirit are able to do so because they discover something about a higher power that is, in fact, the source of their achievement.

Jesus was not a self-help guru. His message was not, "You can do it!" He recognized the scope of human sin, weakness, and failure. He had compassion on those who had been beaten down by the cruelty of life. But he also knew the power of God. Freely granting forgiveness and healing to those who were trapped in their brokenness, he called upon the Spirit to make them new. "For mortals," he said that many things are impossible; but "for God all things are possible" (Mark 10:27). Whenever he healed, whenever he performed a miracle, whenever he had to face down a demonic possession, he lifted his eyes to heaven, collected his spirit within him, and called upon God to enter the hopelessness of the person before him. God responded, and brought new life.

In the Garden of Gethsemane, Jesus collapsed, as any of us would, before the horror of what was inevitably coming. He begged, "Let this cup pass from me. I cannot do this. I cannot endure what is before me. But with you, all things are possible." Then he lifted his eyes to heaven, collected his spirit within him, and called upon the Spirit to enter his hopelessness and do what he could not do: "Nevertheless," he prayed, "not my will, but yours be done. For while the spirit is willing, the flesh is weak" (see Mark 14; Matthew 26; Luke 22). Jesus himself surrendered. He asked God to do what he could not do.

If even Jesus had to do this, how much more do we. There are many things we can do, many accomplishments we can reach and many obstacles we can overcome. God has given us tremendous power in our will, our creativity, and our determination. But there are times when these human capacities are not enough. We run out of ideas, we lose our will, we find that we just can't do it. Even Superman had to deal with kryptonite. Even Samson was powerless without his hair.

Faith is a matter of moving into a region where we are not in control and then trusting anyway. We do not know if things will turn out the way we envision them; we do not know if God will heal us physically, transform our failure into success, or make our problems go away. When we call upon God's help, the only things we do know is that we cannot heal ourselves, we cannot make our failure into a success, we cannot make our problems go away. We also know, in faith, that God is good. These two things—our helplessness and God's goodness—are the only things we know. They are the only things we need to know.

Recently in our parish, we struggled with a fairly serious drop in our income. We did everything we could to address the congregation about this, we examined what could be improved in our ministries, we cut the budget. Some of us laid awake at night wondering if this would result in staff layoffs, and the resultant stress of fewer people having to work even harder. Finally I got to a point where I realized that beyond what we were currently doing, I could not control the outcome. It dawned on me that no matter what happened, God would be good to us. We would be shown a way forward, even with less money and fewer staff, and that good things would come out of whatever happened.

In faith, then, we place our trust in God's goodness. What is this trust like? How do we surrender? For me, there is an almost physical sensation about it, now familiar to me after years of practice. It is as if when I am struggling with something on my own there is this engine driving my will, my worries, my efforts. If I can just worry and try hard enough, I'll figure it out; I'll get through this. But when the engine that drives this anxious effort runs out of gas, I find myself just sitting there, as if on the floor of a room filled with the debris of dashed hope. Just sitting there, I sink physically into the stark reality of the situation: I cannot do this. I feel very still both mentally and physically, as I am reduced to nothing.

And yet paradoxically, when this physical sensation takes

over, another kind of hope stirs, one that is not linked to my being able to work it all out. In this giving up, there is an odd sense of relief. Turning to God, I say with all my being, "I cannot do this. I don't even know what needs to happen here. But you do. Please enter in here, and grant me the grace to get out of the way, to trust, to walk forward in faith. You will do what needs to be done. Give me patience, so that I may not force the issue. I place it all in your hands."

Blind to the future, unable to envision new life, we nevertheless step forward into the unknown, holding God's hand, trusting, like a child. It is the only thing we can do. It is always hard to do it; it never gets easy. But the amazing thing is, when we do this hard thing, there begins to stir within and around us a power that is not our own. Insights come to us. People around us shift their positions. We listen more carefully, and a way forward begins to show itself. A sense of rightness begins to strengthen in our gut. Coincidences take place. As Michael Ramsey, the former Archbishop of Canterbury, used to say, "I'm not sure about miracles, but I do know that when I don't pray, there don't seem to be as many coincidences in my life."

All of this takes place over a period of time, and neither its schedule nor outcome can be forced. We must settle into a reflective, contemplative time of listening, actively watching, waiting, being ready to respond. Having surrendered, having hit the limitations of our human capacity, we then must let go and let God. But this letting go and letting God is hardly passive at this point. Surrender to grace is not like surrendering in defeat. It is active, watchful, attentive, willing to be taken forward beyond the point where we are stuck. It is a state of expectation, where we invite God to become active in us. And yet it is not forced; it is not willful.

There are times when human ingenuity, determination, and skill bring about wonderful things. There are other times when none of these things work. In these times of human failure, we must develop the capacity for attunement to divine grace. Jesus did. We too must learn to understand only this: We are helpless on our own, but God is good. No matter what we can or cannot imagine about the situation we find ourselves in, God is good and will bring forth good. The good that comes may not be what we had hoped for, but it will be the right thing, the thing that brings new life to all concerned. On this we can rely.